. A HISTORY LOVER'S .
GUIDE TO
MINNEAPOLIS

A HISTORY LOVER'S
GUIDE TO
MINNEAPOLIS

SHERMAN WICK & HOLLY DAY

THE
History
PRESS

Published by The History Press
Charleston, SC
www.historypress.com

Cover images from the Library of Congress. All other photos by Sherman Wick.

First published 2019

Manufactured in the United States

ISBN 9781467141932

Library of Congress Control Number: 2019913833

Notice: The information in this book is true and complete to the best of our knowledge. It is offered without guarantee on the part of the authors or The History Press. The authors and The History Press disclaim all liability in connection with the use of this book.

To our mothers, Rita and Elvy.

CONTENTS

PREFACE

Minneapolis is a city of seasons. Regardless of the extremes of the weather, events are paramount and celebrated amid the festive chill and persistent flurries of the annual Holidazzle or the sultriness midsummer of the Aquatennial. The city's landmarks define the topography of Minneapolis—the Chain of Lakes, Spoonbridge and Cherry, the Stone Arch Bridge, the Hennepin Avenue Bridge, the Foshay Tower and the IDS Center—and cast shadows throughout the "City of Lakes" or the "Mill City." For Minneapolis, both municipal mottos reveal the city's history.

The water of the powerful Mississippi River runs throughout the historical genesis of Minneapolis. Surpassing St. Louis in flour production was impossible without the Falls of St. Anthony, a seemingly infinite natural hydrological power source. But the unattainable goal was accomplished in 1880. Minneapolis prevailed—a position retained for fifty years. Moreover, Minneapolis, in the 1870s, exceeded St. Paul in manufacturing. Minneapolis became the most populous city in the Upper Midwest.

I arrived in Minneapolis to attend the University of Minnesota almost thirty years ago. And Minneapolis was the place to be, for me, with the recently defunct Hüsker Dü and the legendary Replacements. Holly came here on a job offer that fell through and stayed because she had family in the area. Together, we've written several books about Minneapolis and nearby St. Paul.

At the end of each chapter, "Your Guide to History" is arranged alphabetically except in some obvious cases for convenience.

This book would be impossible without the resources available at the Minneapolis Central Library and the Minnesota Historical Society.

1
MILL CITY TO CITY OF LAKES

Before steam power was fully developed, the Falls of St. Anthony, the sole waterfall on the Mississippi River, provided the chief source of energy in the region. The duality of the Falls, both as a natural attraction and as an energy resource, recalibrated increasingly to the latter.

The Falls attracted explorers and travelers with its astonishing riverine beauty. One noteworthy traveler was Henry David Thoreau (1807–1862). Afflicted with tuberculosis, commonly known as "consumption," he would die the following year. When Thoreau visited, accompanied by botanist Horace Mann Jr., the nineteen-year-old son of "the Father of the American education," the Falls of St. Anthony's natural beauty was uncompromised. The year 1861 was pivotal, just before the Civil War and after the Panic of 1857, which had destroyed the local and national economy. The trip was Thoreau's longest journey—over 3,500 miles. Thoreau was an influential leader of the Transcendentalist movement that began in the 1820s and 1830s, and his philosophy was influenced by Platonism, romanticism and Kantian philosophy. The poet, philosopher and essayist never formally wrote about the area. But he did draft journals and letters while traveling with state geologist Dr. Charles Anderson.

In March 1935, John T. Flanagan wrote in *Minnesota History Magazine*, "Together they roamed through the woods and around the shores of Lake Calhoun, botanizing and culling specimens of plant and animal life." Thoreau enjoyed the grandeur of the lakes while also noting the prodigious profusion of mosquitoes and ticks despite his perspective emphasizing

Mill City Museum.

common space over commodity and property. "It is obvious that Thoreau viewed the settlements along the upper Mississippi not as hamlets struggling to achieve fame and prosperity, but as happy hunting grounds for naturalist and wanderer who had hitherto been limited to a different terrain with other flora and fauna," wrote Flanagan.

Thoreau hoped to chronicle the natural elegance of the Falls of St. Anthony. But he failed to consult the local Native Americans—the Dakota and the Ojibwe. In the aftermath of the Dakota War, the Dakota and Ojibwe were exiled to Nebraska and South Dakota after the public hanging of thirty-eight Dakota in Mankato on December 26, 1862. The forced removal of the Native Americans opened the falls for lumber milling. Over decades, industrialization was an ongoing process. The milling elites, first, turned away from the river to the lakes, and the Mill City ascended as the nation's flour milling center. The islands around the falls were modified, reshaped or—in the case of Spirit Island—eventually erased from the map.

Spirit Island, or Wanagiyata to the Dakota, was located north of the old Lower Bridge (1857–1934) immediately downriver from the Stone Arch Bridge. Before settlement, the Army Corps of Engineers viewed Spirit Island as a "channel obstruction" to the falls. Composed physically of a St. Peter sandstone base with a limestone cap, the island was eroded away by industrial use.

Jonathan Carver described the island in *Travels Through America 1766–1768*: "At a little distance below the Falls stands a small island of about an acre and a half on which grow a great number of oak trees, every branch of which, able to support the weight, was full of eagles nests." In 1849, Swedish novelist and feminist Fredrika Bremer also discussed the significance of Spirit Island. After she visited St. Anthony, even if she shared some of the racist views of the time, she did appreciate the culture of the American Indians.

First St. Anthony and then Minneapolis were platted on the river. Sawmilling and, later, flour milling built the two cities that merged in 1872. Successive waves of immigrants arrived to fill jobs in the flourishing milling and numerous allied industrial fields. The city's population swelled while reestablished boundaries expanded. From 1880 to 1930, Minneapolis quickly claimed the position of commercial and cultural capital of the Upper Midwest.

Spirit Island continued to be mined away, while Cataract and Upton Islands also vanished with navigation improvement projects by the Army Corps of Engineers at the Upper Mississippi Harbor. Spirit Island's disappearance

The Falls of St. Anthony and the old Mill District.

was chronicled in the *Hennepin County History Magazine* in the spring 1960 issue, while the history was bereft of the American Indians' story.

In the decades before urban renewal, the vicinity of the falls was largely industrial. However, Nicollet Island was forty acres of residences, commercial and industrial buildings and De La Salle High School. The Lower Dam submerged Cataract Island. Finally, the fifteen acres of Hennepin Island was, as *Hennepin County History Magazine*, said, "so cut up that one could hardly tell that it was once a beautiful wooded island."

After almost a century of construction, the Mississippi River above the falls opened for navigation on September 21, 1963. Barges and ships traveled through the locks near the falls for fifty-plus years. But, oddly

Mill Ruins Park.

Downtown Minneapolis from the Number 9 Bridge.

Nice Ride bikes.

enough, it was the threat of "invasive carp" that closed the Upper St. Anthony lock on June 10, 2015.

Betsy Doermann was interviewed by Linda Mack, veteran *Minneapolis Star Tribune* architecture critic, after a successful career at the Minnesota Historical Society and the St. Anthony Falls Heritage Board for the Minneapolis Riverfront Redevelopment Oral History Project (MRROHP) in 2008. Doermann recalled a public meeting at a library and a discussion about the future of the Minneapolis riverfront. A man, she recalled a Northwestern Airlines pilot, suggested, "We've got to change the mindset of the city so that its license plates don't say 'City of Lakes,'" but say, 'City of River and Lakes.'" Minneapolis should be renamed the "City of River and Lakes," not only the "City of Lakes." But cleaning up the Minneapolis Central Riverfront was decades in the making.

Finally, the transformation of the Minneapolis riverfront became a reality in the last decade of twentieth and into the twenty-first century. Today, Minneapolis truly is the "City of River and Lakes."

YOUR GUIDE TO HISTORY

Metro Transit bus and light rail information is available at the handy website www.metrotransit.org

Mill City Museum

704 2nd Street S
Minneapolis, MN 55401
(612) 341-7555
www.mnhs.org/millcity
$12 adults, $10 seniors and students, $6 children 5–17, children 4 and under free

Mill City Museum is built within the ruins of the Washburn "A" Mill, the flagship mill of the Washburn-Crosby Company. (later General Mills). It was the largest and most technologically advanced flour mill in the world when it was completed in 1880 and was a major flour producer until it closed in 1965.

Mill Ruins Park

102 Portland Avenue S
Minneapolis, MN 55401
(612) 230-6400
www.minneapolisparks.org

Mill Ruins Park lies within the St. Anthony Falls Historic District and is listed in the National Register of Historic Places. The history of the area can be seen in the now-exposed historic walls and waterpower features.

Minneapolis Queen

Boarding: Bohemian Flats Park
2150 West River Parkway S.
Minneapolis, MN 55454
(952) 474-8058
www.twincitiescruises.com
$21 per adult, $12 child

The *Minneapolis Queen* takes groups of sightseers along the southern route of the Grand Rounds Scenic Byway and Heritage Trail system, the University of Minnesota Campus riverfront, under the 35W Bridge, and through the lower St. Anthony Falls Lock system, offering a unique perspective of both St. Anthony Falls and the downtown Minneapolis skyline. Food and drink can be purchased during the tour.

Minneapolis Water Taxi

mplswatertaxi.com
$60 to $90 for up to six people

The Minneapolis Water Taxi takes passengers on an hour-long cruise on the shores of the Mississippi. The nesting areas of blue herons, geese and ducks can be seen during the cruise, as well as much of the elusive wildlife that frequents beaches along the river.

Nice Ride Minnesota

www.niceridemn.com

Since 2010, the nonprofit Nice Ride Minnesota has provided a seasonal bike sharing service in Minneapolis.

***

For a general overview of Minneapolis, these are the greatest resources:
    Minneapolis city website, www.ci.minneapolis.mn.us
    Minneapolis Park Board, www.minneapolisparks.org

Minnesota Historical Society

345 Kellogg Boulevard W
Saint Paul, MN 55102
(651) 259-3000
mnhs.org

Minneapolis Visitors Information

505 Nicollet Mall Suite 100
(612) 397-9275
Minneapolis.org

U.S. Army Corps of Engineers at Falls of St. Anthony

Upper St. Anthony Falls Lock and Dam
1 Portland Avenue
Minneapolis, MN 55454

2

ST. ANTHONY FALLS

NATIVE AMERICANS, EXPLORERS, PIONEERS AND SETTLERS

The Falls of St. Anthony attracted the American Indians with abundant game, foraging, natural beauty and spirituality. Much later, European Americans observed the falls' splendor but were compelled by the hydrological power. The Falls of St. Anthony descent is the greatest on the Mississippi River between Minneapolis and St. Paul—more than one hundred feet in less than fifteen miles. It is also the greatest descent in "the gorge" between the Falls of St. Anthony and Fort Snelling. For twelve centuries Native Americans lived at or around the falls, but the archaeological records are lacking besides fluted points (Clovis and Folsom) and unfluted spear points (Plano).

The geological history of the Falls of St. Anthony's began in the Paleozoic era, 500 million years ago. The Twin Cities Basin, the local bedrock depression, is composed of sedimentary rock and glacial drift. The Ordovician-period sea comprises the three uppermost layers of strata, containing Platteville limestone, St. Peter sandstone and Glenwood shale. The limestone sheath is only a couple feet thick at St. Anthony, but it is approximately sixteen feet thick in Southeast Minneapolis. When the Glacial River Warren cut through the layer of Platteville limestone, the falls were approximately 10,000 years old.

At the cataract, the dichotomy between unharnessed nature and serenity mirrored that of natural beauty and waterpower energy. The falls—despite its scenic appearance—was difficult to transform into a transportation waterway. The Army Corps of Engineers were unable to complete the task

Minnehaha Creek at Ford Dam.

until 1963. At the same time, the falls utility as an energy source for milling ended. Lucile M. Kane wrote in the article "Rivalry for the River: The Twin Cities and the Mississippi": "Ironically, it was the falls that had created the barrier between Minneapolis and unimpeded navigation." The turbulent and rocky waters terrified both travelers and steamboat captains.

In 1680, the Dakota occupied land from Mille Lacs to St. Anthony Falls. In the eighteenth and early nineteenth centuries, the Dakota were encroached on by the Ojibwe, who moved west in response to the fur traders and settlers in the East. The Dakota occupied territory around the present-day Twin Cities and the Ojibwe the land that extended to the Mississippi River headwaters and east. The Dakota called the land they occupied Mni Sota Makoce, or "the land where the waters are so clear they reflect the clouds." Gwen Westerman and Bruce White related the cultural differences between the Europeans and Native Americans: "For Dakota people, stories are often tied to places in the landscape and the skies rather than to groups of people or specific bands, which were fluid and mobile." The Dakota were not a nomadic people, but rather migrated seasonally. The arrival of Europeans changed the American Indians' world gradually, at first.

After European women settled in the region, Métis (descendants of Native Americans and Europeans) women's status changed. Mary Lethert

Chief Little Crow Mask by Ed Archie Noisecat.

Wingerd said in *North Country*, they "precipitated a profound shift in the social status of interracial relations." For economic and social reasons, fur traders from France, Britain and Métis married American Indians. American Indian women such as Jane Lamont, Mary Taliaferro, Elizabeth Williams and Nancy Eastman married fur traders in common-law marriage or *à la façon du pays*.

On the frontier, as William D. Green wrote in *A Peculiar Imbalance*, that "racial intermingling" was tolerated. "The social convention of racism did not exist." In a society where existence was only possible with the peaceful coexistence with Native Americans, for white fur traders, as Green said, "Whiteness for its own sake…was hardly a distinction warranting the power to exclude."

Native American social and moral structure allowed for greater gender fluidity. The *berdache*—or "Two Spirits"—was an example. These individuals were considered men/women who served important roles in society. Ozaawindib was an Ojibwe near Leech Lake who also was a berdache, and they were so common that they appeared in one of George Catlin's paintings, *Dance to the Berdache*. Stewart Van Cleve said in *Land of 10,000 Loves: A History of Queer Minnesota*, "Native American civilizations developed diverse sexualities, permitted and even encouraged gender variation, and developed sophisticated social structures long before Europeans arrived in the 'New World.'"

The division of labor was another hurdle of cultural contention between European settlers and the Native Americans. Ojibwe and the Dakota considered farming women's work: men hunted while women tilled the fields. This misunderstanding was a major obstacle in relations. Many settlers believed that American Indian men were indolent because they did not want to farm.

Native Americans' cultural perspective, however, went far beyond gender fluidity and gender roles. And, thus, they were misunderstood by Europeans. Annette Atkins said in *Creating Minnesota: A History from the Inside Out*, "The Europeans made a common ahistorical mistake: feeling (and then presuming it to be fact) that everything that occurred before their own appearance was flat and static and that the most important things have ever happened were occurring in their own lifetimes."

The Dakota named the Falls of St. Anthony Haha Tanka, or "big waterfall"; Minirara, or "curling water"; O-Wa-Mni, "whirlpool," or Owahenah, "falling water." They also respected "the spirit of waters" by praying to Oanktehi, who was below the falls. John O. Anfinson wrote in "12,000 Years at St. Anthony Falls," "Some Dakota bands lived at, near, or within a few hours of the falls when American explorers and settlers arrived in the nineteenth century. The Dakota tapped sugar maples on Nicollet Island. Cloud Man, who had a village at Bde Maka Ska, occasionally camped at the falls. Good Road's band of about 10 tipis sometimes gathered near what is now downtown Minneapolis."

In July 1680, the French Franciscan friar and explorer Father Louis Hennepin (1626–1704) "discovered" the Upper Mississippi River and the Falls of St. Anthony. He was held captive by the Dakota near Lake Pepin while on an expedition for Sieur de La Salle with Antoine Auguelle led by Michel Accault (also spelled Ako, or Aco). On April 11, 1680, he arrived at the Falls of St. Anthony, the first European American to visit and to chronicle his adventure.

Hennepin, baptized in Ath, Belgium, penned a travelogue and history of his journey. Hennepin's style closely resembled Claude Bernou's, and historians have questioned whether Hennepin plagiarized him. Nevertheless, throughout Europe, Hennepin's *Descriptions of Louisiana* (1683) received adulation for his vivid descriptions of the Falls of St. Anthony, "The waterfall is forty or fifty feet high and has a small rocky island, shaped like a pyramid, in the center." His account was evocatively written but slightly exaggerated, especially involving the Falls of St. Anthony, "Navigation is interrupted ten or twelve leagues upstream by a waterfall. I named it the Falls of St. Anthony of Padua in gratitude for favors God did me through the intercession of that great saint, whom we chose as patron and protector of all our enterprises." There is also the matter of audacity, and ethnocentrism, while naming the falls as a captive. Still, Hennepin was the first, and he set the European precedent of recognizing the falls' commercial potential.

Jonathan Carver (1710–1780) of Weymouth, Massachusetts, served in the Massachusetts militia during the French and Indian War. Later, he traveled through the old Northwest from 1766 through 1768. He wrote *Travels Through North America 1766–1768*, first published in 1788. On August 26, 1766, his voyage began at Michilimackinac, Michigan. He traveled to Green Bay and the Fox and Wisconsin Rivers before departing for the Mississippi River and the Falls of St. Anthony. Carver called the falls and the river an "astonishing work of nature."

Carver was the first American explorer to visit the Falls of St. Anthony. "The country around the Falls is extremely beautiful," he wrote. "It is not an uninterrupted plain where the eye finds no relief, but composed of many gentle ascents, which in the summer are covered with the finest verdure, and interspersed with little groves, that give a pleasing variety to the prospect. On the whole, when the Falls are included, which may be seen at the distance of four miles, a more pleasing and picturesque view cannot, I believe, be found throughout the universe."

In 1805, Zebulon M. Pike explored the Falls of St. Anthony. As a member of the U.S military, he engaged in Indian wars and promoting settlement, and his prose described the falls not in terms of natural beauty but rather of economic opportunity. He signed a treaty with the Dakota securing a nine-mile strip on both sides of the Mississippi River from the confluence with the Minnesota River (later Fort Snelling) to the Falls of St. Anthony. During negotiations, alcohol was profligately distributed to facilitate the sale. Land was purchased for 1.25 cents per acre, but after the War of 1812, the Northwest was not settled for decades.

The Ojibwe and Dakota treaties purchased the land and timber between the Mississippi and St. Croix Rivers, with the tribes retaining hunting rights. Pike estimated the land's value at $200,000. The U.S. Senate grossly undervalued the property at a mere $2,000.

Settlement hinged on treaty ratification on both sides of the Mississippi River in St. Anthony and Minneapolis. As Kathy Davis Graves and Elizabeth Ebbott wrote in *Indians in Minnesota*, "The treaty process and the ultimate taking of the land and resources from Indians is a sordid chapter in European and American history. Probably no treaty was honestly or fairly handled; frauds, abuses, and cheating characterized the process."

Stephen H. Long's U.S. government mission entailed selecting a site for a fort on the military reservation negotiated by Pike. On July 17, 1817, he chose the confluence of the St. Peter (later, Minnesota) River and the Mississippi River for siting the fort. Fort Snelling was completed to protect the prime location in 1822. In *The Northern Expedition of Stephen H. Long, the Journals of 1817 and 1823 and Related Documents*, Long wrote, "The Place where we encamped last night needed no embellishments to render it romantic in the highest degree. The banks on both sides of the river are about 100 [50] feet high, decorated with Trees and shrubbery of various kinds. The Post Oak, Hickory, Walnut, Lynden, Sugar tree, White birch, & the American Box, also various evergreens, such as the pine, cedar, juniper &c. added their embellishments to the scene." Furthermore, he named and detailed the variety of fruit trees. He exhaustively catalogued nature, but with economic advancement as the raison d'être. In 1823, Long's second expedition to Minnesota occurred. He named Lake Calhoun (Bde Maka Ska) after the secretary of war in President James Monroe's administration. Giacomo C. Beltrami (1779–1843) traveled with Long to Fort Snelling, then Fort St. Anthony, in 1823. The aristocratic Italian émigré sought the source of the Mississippi River but failed.

For four years, Joseph N. Nicollet (1786–1843) studied Minnesota's geology and resources. The cartographer and explorer drew topographic maps. A native Frenchman, he settled in the United States in 1838. On expeditions, he mapped Minnesota's and the Dakotas' rivers, most importantly, the hydrological basin of the Upper Mississippi River at St. Anthony Falls. After two missions for the U.S. government in 1838 and 1839, Nicollet's greatest accomplishment was a detailed map in 1843. The map informed and influenced government officials' settlement decisions in Washington, D.C.

On each expedition, explorers estimated the Falls of St. Anthony's height. To impress investors and settlers, the explorers embellished on the hydrological potential. Exaggeration was common, but in time, no one questioned the latent power of the only falls on the Mississippi River. The historical estimates of the falls height were: in 1680, Hennepin, forty to sixty feet; in 1700, Jean Penicaut averred; in 1766, Jonathan Carver posited twenty-nine feet; in 1805, Zebulon Pike estimated sixteen and a half feet; and in 1817, Stephen Long agreed, sixteen and a half feet. Hennepin's estimate was accurate when factoring in the rapids' drop below the falls.

Bde Maka Ska.

Regardless, in the four-thousand-foot descent below the falls, there is a fifty-eight-foot drop. The Falls of St. Anthony's power potential attracted settlers to the cataract while the federal government also compelled movement. As Jocelyn Wills in "Boosters, Hustlers, and Speculators" noted, "The land ordinances of 1784 and 1785 set the stage for private real estate and entrepreneurial undertakings for those who ventured to Minnesota during the 1830s and 1840s."

Before Europeans arrived, relations with American Indians centered on the fur trade. The collapse of the fur trade, the movement of settlers west and the soldiers at Fort Snelling were key factors in the eventual signing of treaties that opened St. Anthony—the east side of the Mississippi River. Soldiers received inside information about treaties signed in D.C. via steamboats. However, active service soldiers were ineligible to stake claims, but a former soldier staked the first claim.

He was Franklin Steele. In 1813, he was born in Chester, Pennsylvania. He met James Buchanan, the future president, while working at the post office. According to Marion D. Shutter, in *History of Minneapolis*, he encountered another president. Steele was "advised by Andrew Jackson, then President of the United States, to seek his future in the West." Stevens also reported that Steele, as a young man, traveled to Washington, D.C., from Pennsylvania with a gift from a youth group. Other historians question the veracity of this story. But Stevens went further and asserted Jackson advised Steele to resettle in the prosperous Minnesota lands.

Steele set out to claim the first available land. In 1856, John H. Stevens addressed the Lyceum, "The day he landed at Fort Snelling, the Indians had concluded a treaty with the whites by whom St. Croix Falls were ceded to the latter. Mr. Steele went over; liked the place, made a claim, hired a large crew of men, put Calvin A. Tuttle, Esq., now of St. Anthony, at their head, and commenced in earnest to build mills." Steele was appointed sutler for the U.S. Army at Fort Snelling. He "disposed" of the St. Croix Fall claim.

News arrived on the steamboat *Palmyra*. The treaty was ratified on July 15, 1838. At Fort Snelling, Major Joseph Plympton along with Captain Martin Scott attempted claiming lands. Steele outwitted Plympton, who appeared on July 16, 1836, and accused Steele of jumping his claim. It was located near the present-day Pillsbury "A" Mill. Steele had the law on his side, as active servicemen were excluded from staking claims.

In the first decade, commercial development of St. Anthony was slow. Steele returned, repeatedly, to the East for financing. After "improving" his claim, he hired a man named La Grue and his wife as caretakers in July 1836. One day, La Grue went fishing and afterward found Mrs. La Grue had perished in a fire. Steele then hired Charles Lantry, a French Canadian, to hold his claim. But Lantry briefly abandoned the land, and Theodore Menk (alternately spelled Mink) jumped Steele's claim. Steele paid $200 cash plus $100 worth of goods to Menk for his claim. Lantry was fired.

Steele's claim on the east side of St. Anthony was expanded to 332 acres that included Nicollet Island. He had overextended his finances. In 1846, Steele was backed by eastern money: Caleb Cushing and Robert Rantoul Jr., both Massachusetts lawyers and politicians. Benjamin, the brother of William Cheever of then nearby Cheevertown, also brokered financial support. But by 1848, all financiers had pulled out of deals. Green said in *A Peculiar Imbalance*, "When Steele began having difficulties with his business partners in the East, he had trouble developing the holdings." The *St. Anthony Express* editorialized about Steele's financial woes as early as 1851. Steele turned to Arnold W. Taylor of Dorchester. Taylor proved more erratic, with perpetual harassment and litigation. Steele was unable to buy out Taylor until 1852. He continued lawsuits, but Steele prevailed in an appeal case.

In 1848, Steele built his sawmill. Two more opened in 1849. By 1856, sawmilling production skyrocketed: twelve million board feet was produced in St. Anthony and Minneapolis. Enterprising writers like Nathan H. Parker shared their experience with hyperbolic exaggeration to encourage settlement in *The Minnesota Handbook* (1856–57). He described Minneapolis as a "town which, for beauty of location and rapidity of growth, is scarcely excelled by any other in the Territory."

The city of St. Anthony Falls (the Falls was later dropped) was organized in 1849. In 1848, William R. Marshall, originally of Missouri and later of St. Paul, surveyed the original 12½-block plat with streets that ran roughly parallel with avenues at approximate right angles. The lots were 66 feet wide and 16 feet deep. Marshall also platted the Pierre Bottineau claim in the vicinity of Boom Island, and Cheevertown, with a hotel, stagecoach route on the territorial road to St. Paul and an observatory. The tourist attraction said "pay a dime and climb." But Cheevertown's 25 acres were sold to the University of Minnesota regents for $6,000 for a campus in 1854. In 1855, the city of St. Anthony was organized when the Bottineau and Cheever plats were added to Steele's.

Henry T. Welles was elected the first mayor of St. Anthony on April 2, 1855. The population was 2,195. Mrs. Anna Hennes Huston offered a rustic anecdote from her youth in *Old Rail Fence Corners: Frontier Tales Told by Minnesota Pioneers*, edited by Lucy Leavenworth Wilder Morris: "I was only a

Old St. Anthony.

tiny tot but used to go with my brother along a path by the river to find our cow. We usually found her in the basement of the University."

Many settlers arrived for health benefits, including John H. Stevens and Charles M. Loring. John W. Bond wrote in *Minnesota and Its Resources* (1853), "From a residence of over six years in Minnesota, I can safely say that the atmosphere is more pure, pleasant, and healthful, than any other I have ever breathed on the continent of North or South America." In the *Minnesota Guide*, J.F. Williams concurred: "The climate is the principal boast of Minnesota. It is claimed to be 'the healthiest in the world.' The testimony of thousands of cured invalids, and the experience of and statistics of twenty years, confirm this." The pamphlet also exaggerated the weather: "The popular impression that the further north you go the colder it gets, is an erroneous one." Bond also said, "The most remarkable characteristic of winter of Minnesota, is its great dryness—there being an almost total absence of rain or moisture." Apparently, he missed the snow during his visit.

Ella S. Godley arrived in Minneapolis in 1856. She accurately described the weather in *Old Rail Fence Corners*: "No one who was used to an eastern climate had any idea how to dress out here when they first came. I wore hoops and a low necked waist just as other little girls did. I can remember the discussion that took place before merino sack was made for me. I don't remember whether I was supposed to be showing the white feather if I surrendered to the climate and covered my poor little bare neck or whether I would be too out of style." Furthermore, Mrs. Godley recalled an errand in which she purchased vinegar in twenty-below weather but returned with a frozen bottle.

Explaining away frigid winter weather was commonplace by boosters promoting settlement, such as the complete mumbo-jumbo dispensed by J.W. McClung in 1870 for *Minnesota as It Is*. "Why we do not feel the cold?" He answered, "A moist atmosphere is a conductor…and a sensation of chilliness is rare, even in the coldest winter."

Despite disingenuous efforts to attract settlers, there were opportunities aplenty in the fledgling city. Water power was inexhaustible to industrial development—and also a natural wonder. The *St. Anthony Express* wrote on July 1, 1854, in the article "Logs on the Falls," "A. Godfrey is now successfully engaged in hauling off the jam of logs on the Falls. He uses the waterpower for this purpose." The role of the falls and the Mississippi River was repeatedly revisited. *The Minnesota Handbook* called the falls "The crowning glory of the northeast," and said, "These falls have been a point of attraction for years past, and will ever continue to be. The number of visitors will annually increase, just in proportion as the beauty and magnificence of the scenery on the upper Mississippi, and the grandeur of these cataracts." E.S. Seymour, in *Sketches of Minnesota* (1850), predicted, "Water power in Minnesota is abundant, but this at St. Anthony is so extensive, and so favorably situated, that it will invite a concentration of mechanical talent, and of population; whereby the necessary facilities for profitable manufacturing will be abundantly afforded." Loring desired a New England on the prairie. The park system was central to such a development. Bond and others promoting settlement wanted New Englanders as well, as he said of St. Anthony in 1853, "[It] will soon contain a large population of retired people of substance, as well as invalids and people of fortune, desiring literary privilege in a retired beautiful town."

In 1856, with East Coast capital investment, Steele started the St. Anthony Falls Water Power Company. In 1858, his designs expanded when he purchased the Fort Snelling reservation for the development of the expanding city—he paid $30,000 of the $90,000 price. He also outraged local citizens and politicians, especially of the Whig and nascent Republican ranks. But in that year, Minnesota received statehood and the frontier moved west, where new forts were constructed. Regardless, the United States leased the fort during the Civil War.

But Steele failed. His grandiose plans lacked feasibility and financial backing. By 1869, the west side of the river increasingly outpaced Steele; the Minneapolis Mill Company milled twice as much lumber. And in 1871, there were twenty-five factories: ten flour mills, seven sawmills, two woolen, cotton, paper, ironworks, a sash mill, a planing mill and a railroad machine shop—all were water-powered.

In 1875, Steele sold his interest in the St. Anthony Falls Water Power Company to Richard and Samuel Chute and Frederick Butterfield. He experienced further financial woes. However, across the river, downtown Minneapolis, centered on Bridge Square, was in full ascent.

Finally, Chute and Butterfield sold all St. Anthony Falls Water Power to the St. Paul, Minneapolis & Manitoba Railway Company, affiliated with James J. Hill, in 1880. But Hill's primary interest was the right of way for a bridge—the future Stone Arch Bridge.

Between 1876 and 1880, the Minneapolis Mill Company purchased all sawmills and closed them. They were relocated, considered a waste of water power. Lumber production did not maximize profits. Remaining lumber mills moved upriver to North and Northeast Minneapolis. Lumber milling was lucrative but nowhere near the profits from flour milling. In *Minnesota: A History*, Theodore C. Blegen noted, "By 1869 there were fifteen sawmills at or near the Falls of St. Anthony. The Minneapolis lumber business leaped far beyond that of Stillwater as expansion continued in the 1870s and 1880s. By 1890 Minneapolis, cutting close to a half billion feet, was the premier lumber market not only of Minnesota but of the world."

The first prominent citizens of St. Anthony were a diverse amalgam; each man had a different vision for the city. As a result, within a decade, many had moved on to create the utopia of their dreams elsewhere.

Pierre Bottineau, a Métis, was an original settler in St. Anthony with a lifelong wanderlust. He was born in Pembina, presently in North Dakota, in the Red River region on January 1, 1817. His father was originally from Boston, of Huguenot background, while his mother had the Ojibwe name "The Clear-Sky Woman." Early in life, he was a pathfinder and scout for the failed Selkirk Colony in Manitoba, Canada, and served as scout and messenger for Henry H. Sibley of the American Fur Company. In 1840, he homesteaded near present-day downtown St. Paul. Later, he was a guide for the exploration of Yellowstone Park for the Northern Pacific Railroad. But he also suppressed the Dakota Uprising in 1862.

He settled in St. Anthony in 1846 and later founded Osseo. In the summer of 1958, the *Hennepin County History Magazine* reprinted an article "Pierre Bottineau…the Last Voyageurs" from the October 5, 1895 issue of *Illustrated American*. The magazine eulogized Bottineau: "There has just died near the little town of Red Lake Falls, Minnesota, a man who in a peculiarly personal way linked the earlier part of the century with the present, Pierre Bottineau, the last of the famous scouts and trappers and voyageurs whose lives were so intimately related to progress, as well as the conquest of the West." Bottineau died at eighty-one or possibly eighty-two—the magazine wasn't sure; like many during this time of his background, his exact birth date was uncertain. The magazine continued the tribute, acknowledging his talents; he was "familiar with the leading Indian languages of the region as he was with the paths of the forest."

In 1849, John W. North arrived in St. Anthony from the abolitionist haven of upstate New York. As Green said in *A Peculiar Imbalance*, St. Anthony, then, was "a community of like-minded activists." Like his mentor, congressman, presidential candidate and social reformer Gerrit Smith, North desired the civilization of the East. North was elected to the territorial legislature in 1851.

On July 4, 1854, an antislavery convention met at the Congregational church in St. Anthony with North, Reverend Charles Secombe and Reverend C.G. Ames, while temperance leaders forbade whiskey drinking

The Upton Block.

and gambling until 1855, when liquor licensing was permitted and thirty lumberjacks teemed into the town. John and his wife, Ann, resided first on Nicollet Island and then on University Avenue SE. They dreamed of a genteel and sober eastern town, not a rambunctious mill village. In his book, Green described St. Anthony after the city was platted in 1849: "It was a different community from St. Paul, one based on the enlightenment and reform."

Within two years, a library association, a newspaper and the University of Minnesota were established in the town. A town similar to the city was described by another John Wesley Bond, in "Minnesota and Its Resources," in 1853: "The town of St. Anthony now contains over two thousand inhabitants, and is most beautifully picturesque in its position." North would move on to found Northfield and thereafter continue his travels. But North didn't find the civic life that he wanted, so he moved west, eventually to Riverside, California—the land of wintertime train-delivered oranges—where, later in life, Charles Loring wintered.

When the Norths relocated to Riverside, California, they remembered Christmas in St. Anthony. So, they ventured into a business endeavor that brightened the holidays and became a tradition for decades—Christmas oranges. Before 1841, there were zero commercial orange groves in California. The original oranges planted were imported from China. Between 1860 and 1880, Spain remained the largest producer of oranges, but by 1920, the United States dominated the market.

The Norths' involvement is as unbelievable as a Hollywood screenplay. As Atkins wrote in her book, "The storyline includes subplots about the railroad, commercial agriculture, the birth of advertising, Americanization, the invention of traditional Christmas, and the relationship of Minnesota to many places through this fruit."

In 1869, the Norths founded a "colony" to grow oranges. They envisioned "a better St. Anthony" in the West. In 1878, they planted four trees, and only two survived. In 1907, the trees and their progeny produced an astonishing harvest of ten million oranges. The first train with oranges traveled east in 1877. The oranges were, eventually, distributed in Kansas City, St. Louis, Chicago—and Minneapolis.

Colonel John H. Stevens (1820–1900), of New England stock, was born in the province of Quebec, Canada. By appealing to Franklin Steele's recommendation, he opened the west side of the river with ferryboat service on the military reserve to St. Anthony. He returned from the Mexican-American War prepared to settle in Texas—but first visited Fort Snelling.

The fourth Hennepin Avenue Bridge.

He laid claim to 160 acres. Blegen said about Steele, "His calculating judgment led him in 1849 to suggest to John H. Stevens, his clerk, that it might be good business to get a permit from the War Department to stake a claim on the west bank, above the falls, on lands then part of the military reservation." In 1851, Steele was awarded ferry privileges for ten years, with William Dubay and Edgar Folsom the first to hold the position. However, Captain John Tapper was the most well-known ferryboat driver and later served as toll collector for the first Hennepin Avenue Bridge.

As the first European American settling on the west side of the Mississippi, Stevens was accorded a position of high esteem and frequently gave speeches to civic organizations. When he addressed the Minneapolis Lyceum in 1856, this was apparent. He chronicled arrivals to the fledgling settlement individual by individual. He recalled, "The first settler in Minneapolis was myself. I came here in 1849 and was followed by C.A. Tuttle in 1850, J.P. Miller in 1850." Stevens listed every settler that arrived in Minneapolis through 1852. Many of these dozens of people were pivotal in the development of the city, for example, Charles Hoag. Later, Stevens sold forty acres in Minneapolis and then moved to Glencoe, Minnesota.

In 1855, the city of Minneapolis was incorporated. It had been platted in 1854. Downtown Minneapolis streets, like those in St. Anthony, were oriented to run parallel with the Mississippi River, with later plats following a directional orientation: north, south, east, west, southeast and northeast. By 1855, there were approximately two thousand settlers.

The first Hennepin Avenue Bridge connected the two rising cities. During a frigid weather, the *St. Anthony Express* reported on the "Grand Celebration" and "on the opening of the Mississippi River Wire Suspension Bridge," in the January 27 edition. It had opened the previous Tuesday on January 23, 1855. And "the cold, calm grey of early dawn foretold an auspicious day" for the event when "well-filled sleighs" arrived at the bridge that opened at 1:00 p.m. with over "100 sleighs." The bridge was engineered by a Mr. Griffith. Isaac Atwater was involved in the incorporation of the first Hennepin Avenue Bridge, one of many civic achievements with his imprimatur.

Atwater was a Renaissance man in St. Anthony and later Minneapolis. He arrived from New York in 1850, a graduate of Yale College and law school, and a law partner of John W. North. He served on the school board, the city council and as a founder of the University of Minnesota. He was also editor of the *Express* in 1851. In 1857, he was appointed and confirmed to the Minnesota Supreme Court. The local historian was described by Edward D. Neill in "History of Hennepin County and the City of Minneapolis": "In few men are more rare combinations of talent required, than in pioneers of new countries; invincible courage, enterprise tempered by prudence; promptness and decision united by calm reflection; sagacity combined with enthusiasm, are indispensably requisites."

Dorilus Morrison was the first mayor of Minneapolis after the merger. He was born in Livermore, Maine, in 1814, but sought his fortune in the lumber business in 1854. He spent a year in Stillwater with a fellow Maine lumberman and operated a dry goods store after arriving in St. Anthony. His cousins, the Washburns, were also from Maine. The men made a fortune on lumbering and then diversified into flour milling, banking and subsidizing the public appreciation of fine art. He was also first president of the Minneapolis School Board, a park commissioner and a trustee for the Lakewood Cemetery as well as president of the Northwestern National Bank.

In 1928, Charles Edward Russell captured the rags-to-riches Horatio Algerian myth of the rise of the lumber barons in "A-Rafting on the Mississippi." He described the successful Maine lumbermen:

> *At first, the men that went into the woods were straight out of old American stock, hardy wanderers from Maine or elsewhere in northern New England, avid to make their way in the world but straight, clean and quaintly religious after the school of Jonathan Edwards. Many of them began with nothing but an ax and their two hands and rose by hard work and merit. John Martin and Dorilus Morrison, afterwards among the most respected citizens of Minneapolis, were of this order and beginning.*

Morrison's home—the eight-and-a-half-acre Villa Rosa, became the site of Mia (Minneapolis Institute of Art). It was donated by his son Clinton and stood across the street from the (William D.) Washburn Fair Oaks Park—the former site of the congressman and senator's mansion. Before he was elected, his residence on 24th Avenue S—Villa Rosa—was outside the city limits and was ruled ineligible. Hence, the city limits were expanded—and Morrison was elected mayor. His grandson Clinton summarized his accomplishments in *The Morrisons: Minneapolis Pioneers*: "During his tenure as mayor, Dorilus was involved in the shaping and formation of the water system, fire department, sewage system, police department, and numerous street improvements." In 1915, Elizabeth Washburn died, and the land was acquired as a park—and a beautiful frontage for viewing the art museum.

The Washburn family was distinguished by government service and philanthropy. Several of the eleven Washburn children were prominent politicians: Israel Jr., the governor of Maine and also a member of Congress; Elihu, U.S. secretary of state; and Cadwallader, governor of Wisconsin and a congressman. Plus, Minneapolis's William D. Washburn served in Congress and as a U.S. senator. The Washburn family loathed Free Soilers such as Franklin Steele and Henry M. Rice. This reality caused an early political schism between the east and west bank business interests and played out in the development of the two cities that emerged as one.

Cadwallader C. Washburn recognized the economic value of the west bank of the Mississippi River. But the property was off limits, except for the military reservation, decades before Washburn's involvement on the same site. In 1823, the first saw- and gristmills were constructed by Fort Snelling soldiers on the Mississippi River. In 1819, Lieutenant Colonel Henry Leavenworth began the mills that Josiah Snelling completed construction of between 1821 and 1823.

In 1849, Illinois congressman Robert Smith leased the government mill and sawmill for five years. And like Stevens, he made a 160-acre claim on present-day downtown Minneapolis. His claim was to settle the east side of the Mississippi River. Dorilus Morrison acted for and with a loan from Cadwallader Washburn and eleven others to form the Minneapolis Mill Company. Incorporated in 1856, the company developed water power on the west bank in 1855. The company constructed a dam that met with the St. Anthony Falls Water Power Company on the east side of river. It was completed in 1858. The V-shaped dam channeled the water to the mills on both sides of the river.

The Minneapolis Mill Company also engineered an elaborate canal and waterpower system. In 1857, the canal system commenced as John Anfinson said in his article, "to extend the falls' power to mills located back from the river. Workers broke through the limestone cap and removed the soft, underlying sandstone cap and removed the soft, underlying sandstone to create a canal 14 deep, 50 feet wide, and 215 feet long (later extended and deepened). The canal system included turbine or wheel pits, a labyrinth of underground tunnels, headraces, and tailraces leading off and back into the river, and an open canal. Altogether, the system ran for about three miles. With the boost, by 1869 the west side was producing twice as much lumber as the east."

In the history of St. Anthony, improving navigation was attempted early but with little success. In 1850, the steamer *Lamantine* docked just south of St. Anthony, with great difficulty, at Steele's Landing. The process of improving navigation on the Mississippi River was set in motion. In the

1850s, St. Anthony and Minneapolis lobbied the Minnesota legislature and U.S. Congress for appropriations for the Mississippi River.

After 1856, the falls receded 7.0 feet per year. Only 1,000.0 feet remained before the limestone sheath that protected the falls, and the cataract would be replaced by rapids. Moreover, the mills' growth accelerated the process. On October 24, 1876, *Mississippi Lumberman* noted that the falls receded 640.0 feet between 1852 and 1869—or approximately 35.3 feet per year—and about 100.0 feet per year in 1860s before the apron. To slow the process, the east and west side mill companies collaborated to complete the V-neck dam.

The problems at the falls culminated on October 4, 1867. The Eastman Tunnel collapse spurred repeated attempts at merger. The collapse happened after two thousand feet of tunnel were completed and only five hundred feet remained. The *Stillwater Messenger* underscored the significance of the erosion of the falls on November 10, 1871: "the danger of the Falls and the lack of fixing upon any sure and permanent remedy to the undermining and breaking away of the rocky river bed, has exercised a depressing influence on the business of Minneapolis during the past summer." Furthermore, the paper stated, "It is generally understood that the first alarm in regard to the condition of the Falls arose from a break in the Eastman tunnel under Nicollet Island. This tunnel is excavated under the limestone ledge which constitutes the foundation of the river for about one thousand feet above the crest of the Falls."

In 1861, Wisconsin fur trader and real estate speculator Hercules Dousman from Prairie du Chien, Wisconsin, sold the land on Nicollet Island that he received after mortgage foreclosure on Franklin Steele for a mere $24,000. But another failed attempt failed to expand east side water power—the Chute Tunnel—excavated an enormous cave at Main Street and 4th Avenue SE. It was abandoned in 1864.

William Eastman and John L. Merriam excavated a two-thousand-foot tunnel under the falls from Hennepin Island and Nicollet Island. A portion of Nicollet Island was permanently lost to the Mississippi River. Mills including the Summit Mill were destroyed. Over six years, there were six breaks before the tunnel was completely sealed. The Army Corps of Engineers constructed an underground dike that was four feet thick and forty feet high while two thousand feet long. Eastman's disastrous project caused $1 million in damages.

Lucile M. Kane described the Falls of St. Anthony before the intervention of local waterpower interest and the Army Corps of Engineers in an article: "Into the caldron, the cataract, still retreating, dropped and annual load of rock and sand, until the water-power companies which controlled the falls in the 1860s built a shield to prevent further erosion."

Also, to save the Falls of St. Anthony, there was the impetus for massive federal effort. First, the falls were covered with wood, and then concrete was poured. In 1866, civil engineer Franklin Cook built a wooden apron to alleviate further recession of the falls. In 1870, to preserve navigation, the Army Corps of Engineers received $50,000. The federal government appropriated $615,000 on the concrete apron and bypass channels to prevent further erosion upstream between 1870 and 1884.

Bridge Square was the historic center of Minneapolis. Taking its name from the nearby Hennepin Avenue Bridge along with the Gateway District that developed around, it was the focus of urban renewal. The Gateway developed, later, and though it had no formal boundaries, the district stretched from the Mississippi River in the east to Washington Avenue, 3rd Avenue S and west of Hennepin Avenue. The original downtown Minneapolis experienced the rise and fall—and recent renaissance—of the city.

In 1855, Minneapolis was eight square miles with 210 blocks and 60 intersecting streets. But, as "St. Anthony Falls Rediscovered" stated, most blocks were "figments of the surveyor's imagination." John Borchert, David Gebhard, David Lanegran and Judith A. Martin in *Legacy of Minneapolis* stated that in 1854, St. Anthony was the "center of the retail trade," with thirty-one "small stores." By 1874, the commercial center had shifted to Washington Avenue. The focus moved due south to Nicollet, Hennepin and Washington Avenues in the 1880s.

Bridge Square was at the intersection of Hennepin and Nicollet Avenues. It met with the adjoining North 1st Street and hotels, stores and taverns. Nicollet Avenue follows the trail to Fort Snelling. During the 1850s, Bridge Square was surrounded primarily by residential housing. In 1856, John B. Pomeroy, Bates and Company operated a steam-powered sawmill at Basset Creek. Houses moved farther away from Bridge Square—and especially of the wealthy lumber barons—as the businesses became more concentrated.

Mary Thaler Hale said of Bridge Square, "On either side was a straggling row of one-story stores," and in the center was the Goose Pond. In 1856, Mrs. Charles Godley lived in the city expanding from the Bridge Square, the core. In *Old Rail Fence Corners*, she described the frontier, now the old Warehouse District: "My father, Mr. Scrimgeour, came to Minneapolis in 1855 and built a small home between First and Second Avenue North and 4th Street. When my mother arrived she cried when she saw where her home was to be and said to her husband, as he was cutting hazel brush from around the house, 'You told me I would not have to live in a wilderness if I came here.'" Mrs. Godley also recalled social events in her youth at Bridge Square:

> *A boardwalk six blocks long was built from Bridge Square to Bassett's Hall on First Street North. It was a regular sidewalk, not just two boards laid out lengthwise and held by crosspieces as the other sidewalks were. Our dress parade always took place there. We would walk back and forth untiringly, passing everybody we knew and we knew everybody in town. Instead of taking a girl out driving or to the theatre, a young man would ask, "Won't you go walking on the boardwalk?"*

When Bridge Square was at its apex, U.S. Grant, the future president, visited before his presidency in 1865.

In the 1870s, Bridge Square was the business center. Small wood-frame structures were replaced by brick buildings. The population numbered thirteen thousand in 1870. St. Anthony was hobbled by the Panic of 1857 and the Civil War but had five thousand citizens.

Before a permanent city hall was constructed, municipal business was held at the Pence Opera House. It was located in the heart of Bridge Square at Hennepin Avenue and 2nd Street. On the first and second floors, the three-story building housed commercial businesses, with the opera house on the third floor. For the June 21, 1867 grand opening, ticket prices ranged from one to five dollars.

In 1873, the permanent city hall was constructed in Bridge Square at the intersection of Hennepin and Nicollet Avenues. The city hall was a limestone wedge-shaped building 160 feet long and 20 feet wide at its narrowest. Downtown expanded from the Mississippi River during Bridge Square's golden age. Businesses included S.E. Olson's Dry Goods, the Union Depot, horse cars, the Pence Opera House, T.K. Gray's Drug Store, Mendenhall's Bank, Fish Jones Zoo and the Electric Light Mast—the world's tallest light fixture at 257 feet in 1882. It had eight four-thousand-candlepower lamps. In 1884, thirty-five arc lamps were added in downtown. This local attraction lasted less than a decade. It was replaced by street lighting in 1892. In 1912, Minneapolis General Electric Company became part of Northern States Power Company. In the spring of 1882, Oscar Wilde lectured at the Minneapolis Music Academy in the five-story Nicollet House—later the Nicollet Hotel—and then he appeared in St. Paul.

Minneapolis City Hall.

According to *Old Rail Fence Corners*, Helen Horton arrived in 1856. She described the new neighborhood: "The first home we owned ourselves was at the corner of Ninth Street and Nicollet Avenue. There was only one house in sight, that of Mr. Welles." She continued, "My father had a store at the corner of Helen Street [2nd Avenue S] and Washington Avenue. To reach it from our home at Fourth Street and Second Avenue North, we followed an Indian trail. There was generally a big cow with a bell to turn out from somewhere on it."

David L. Rosheim described the de facto downtown in *The Other Minneapolis; or, the Rise and Fall of the Gateway, the Old Minneapolis Skid Row*. In 1875, "The Gateway was more than important. It was the city. In 1875—it boasted all the amusements, all the four architectural firms, all three artists, eight of eleven banks, nine of eleven cigar stores, ten of twelve clothing stores, nine of eleven dentists, most of the druggists, half of the restaurants, and forty-seven of the fifty-nine saloons." The Gateway eclipsed old St. Anthony, and the old city was slipping into decrepitude. In the same process, the Gateway would gradually decline and follow a similar path at the turn of the twentieth century.

The Gateway District was twenty-five blocks that centered on Hennepin, Washington and Nicollet Avenues. As the city moved away from the increasingly dirty Mississippi River and Bridge Square, the Gateway

Hennepin Avenue Bridge.

declined. Cheap hotels, saloons and employment agencies replaced bookstores and banks.

Bridge Square was also called the "Lower Loop" in later years. By 1912, there was a demolition contract, and a fire soon struck. In 1915, the Beaux-Arts pavilion at the Gateway Park was built on the site. It was Minneapolis's first attempt at urban renewal.

St. Anthony and Minneapolis merged on February 28, 1872. It created ten wards for the first election in 1873. George A. Brackett was elected the first mayor. But there had been several earlier attempts, in 1859 and 1860, when the Union Board of Trade proposed merger. On the day the merger was finally completed, *St. Anthony Falls Democrat* wrote about the Reverend George Chase of the Holy Trinity Church of St. Anthony: "When I first came to this place, I was impressed with the fact the 'Duel City' owed much of its importance and prosperity to lumber." Efforts at unity were made, as the *St. Anthony Falls Democrat* said with the headline "The People's City Movement." Fifty or more "leading citizens on both sides of the river" met at the office of H.T. Welles to select acceptable candidates.

YOUR GUIDE TO HISTORY

Father Hennepin Bluffs Park
420 Main Street SE
Minneapolis, MN 55414
(612) 230-6400
www.minneapolisparks.org

Father Hennepin Bluffs Park was named for Father Louis Hennepin, a Franciscan priest who was the first European to view St. Anthony Falls from the site of the park in 1680 after being captured by the Dakota and brought to the site. Hennepin named the falls for his patron saint, St. Anthony of Padua.

First Bridge Park
1 West River Parkway
Minneapolis, MN 55401
(612) 230-6400
www.minneapolisparks.org

This park is located at the site of the first permanent suspension bridge to span the Mississippi River. The first Hennepin Avenue Bridge linked the east and west banks of the Mississippi River. On January 23, 1855, there was a celebration. Franklin Steele, John H. Stevens and Isaac Atwater formed the bridge company. Nicollet Island was used to shorten the distance of the spans. The Second Hennepin Avenue Suspension Bridge was in use from 1876 to 1890. The third bridge on the site was the Hennepin Avenue Steel Arch Bridge. It lasted until 1989, when the fourth bridge was constructed.

John H. Stevens House
4901 Minnehaha Avenue S
Minneapolis MN 55417
(612) 722-2220
johnhstevenshouse.org
 $3 for adults, $1 for children

John H. Stevens House was the first frame house on the west side of the Mississippi River. Captain John Tapper and Charles Mousseau helped to build the structure. The white one-and-a-half-story house with adjoining kitchen was completed in the winter of 1849–50. At that time, Dakota teepees were often spotted at the future intersection of Hennepin and Nicollet Avenues. In the spring, the Dakotas sugared maple trees on nearby Nicollet Island. The board of commissioners chose the west bank as the county seat. In 1881, the house was relocated because of the Union Railway Station and moved twice before 1896. The original site was near Hennepin Avenue and 1st Street.

In the 1870s, the house moved to 16th Avenue S and 4th Street west of Cedar Avenue. One thousand schoolchildren towed the house with ropes in seven relays to Minnehaha Park on May 28, 1896. The next day's *Minneapolis Tribune* headlines read "All Took a Hand," "School Children Move the Old Stevens House." The paper described the relocation: "The first residence built in Old Minneapolis given a final site at Minnehaha Park—enthusiastic thousands of grade and high school pupils—join hands in the event—rivalry between the Central and South Side Schools breaks in new place."

The park board allowed the Historical Society of St. Anthony to use the house as a headquarters. John S. Pillsbury served as president. Within the house, the name "Minneapolis" was selected. In the 1980s, once again, Stevens House moved a couple hundred feet and the Junior League of Minneapolis restored the historic home. At Minnehaha Park, near the house is the Stevens' Monument, a life-sized bronze statue mounted on a granite pedestal, sculpted by Jacob Fjelde.

Water Power Park

204 Main Street SE
Minneapolis, MN 55414
(612) 230-6400
nps.gov

The designs of this park allowed visitors to walk as close to the Falls of St. Anthony as one possibly could without being in a boat. Interpretive panels describe the reengineering of the falls from a natural cataract into one harnessed for industrial purposes.

St. Anthony Falls is the only natural waterfall on the Mississippi River, carved out roughly twelve thousand years ago by the activity of the glacial River Warren Falls. Over thousands of years, the Falls moved from its original location approximately 4 feet upstream every year (decreasing in size from an estimated 180 feet high to its current height of roughly 16 feet) until it reached its present location in the early nineteenth century, when the Army Corps of Engineers put an artificial cap on it to keep it from disintegrating further.

3

"GATEWAY TO THE NORTHWEST"

THE GRID AND STREET PLAN OF MINNEAPOLIS

In 1854, Colonel John H. Stevens hired Charles Christmas to survey Minneapolis. The street plan of Minneapolis was clearly influenced by New England towns. Eventually, the grid was organized with six directional markers, plus numbered and alphabetical streets or, in Northeast Minneapolis, streets chronologically named after presidents.

Of course, without a permanent name, the establishment of neighborhoods in the city was impossible. According to Marion Shutter in *History of Minneapolis*, commissioners met and attempted to name the city at the John Stevens House on October 21, 1852. Each member had a suggestion for the city: Judge Isaac Atwater liked Hennepin City, Alexander Moore supported Albion and Commissioner Dean was partial to Lowell. Others preferred Brooklyn. Another name bandied about was Addiesville, after "a popular woman" in the town. Winona, or "first born daughter" in Dakota, was also suggested.

Outside of the city, boosters promoted short-lived names for Minneapolis. James Madison Goodhue, publisher of the *Minnesota Pioneer*, strongly lobbied for All Saints. John H. Stevens recollected the detailed process in "Personal Recollections: Minnesota and Its People and Early History of Minneapolis." Stevens wrote,

> *Then the question came up as to what name should be given to the place selected as the county-seat. Commissioner Moore thought Albion would be a proper name. Another commissioner said that, in view of the extensive*

Northeast Minneapolis, home of Art-a-Whirl.

water-power, the name of Lowell would be suggestive, as the power, when improved, would make this place the Lowell of the West. A vote being taken, the name of Albion was selected, and the clerk was directed to so record it. He was further instructed to date all records of the county under the head of "Albion, Hennepin County, Minnesota."

But the city's name was not resolved, as neither Albion nor All Saints were universally supported.

Charles Hoag, a Philadelphia schoolteacher, named Minneapolis. He had a farm on 5th Street and Hennepin Avenue. Hoag wrote to editor George A. Bowman of the *St. Anthony Express*, and his letter was published on November 5, 1852. It was both signed by and proposed the name "Minnehapolis." Hoag had combined Minnehaha and *polis*. Charles Hoag signed the letter "Minnehapolis." He regarded the *St. Anthony Express* as "sort of an exponent of public sentiment." He also commented that for the county seat of Hennepin City, "All Saints" was a "miserable misnomer," "and is applicable to no more than two persons in the vicinity of the falls." Then he said, "The name I propose Minnehapolis, derived from Minne-ha-ha laughing water, with the Greek affix polis, a city, meaning 'laughing water City,' or 'city of the Falls.'" Finally, Hoag offered the one objectionable item: "I spell it with an h which is silent in the pronunciation."

Bowman urged the city leaders to "adopt this beautiful and exceedingly appropriate title," and "do not longer suffer," with "the meaningless and outlandish name of 'All Saints.'"

The editor verbosely averred in the November 12 edition:

> *When the communication proposing this name for the promising town growing up on the other side of the river was last week handed to us we were so much engaged as to have no time to comment. The name is an excellent one, and deserves much favor from the citizens of the capital of Hennepin. No other in our opinion could be chosen that would embody to the same extent the qualities desirable to the name. The h being silent, as our correspondent recommends, and as custom would soon make it, it is poetical and euphonious; the nice adjustment of the Indian minne, with the Greek polis, forms a beautiful compound, and, finally, it is as all names should be when it is possible, admirably descriptive of the locality.*

As Stevens said in *Personal Recollections*, "It was evident that Messrs. Hoag and Bowman had won the victory. It was finally settled at the accidental meeting of most all the citizens at my house, in December, 1852."

Hoag later served as the first superintendent of Hennepin County Schools from 1870 to 1874.

Once the city was named, Minneapolis was first divided east and west. The Mississippi River—and its east and west banks—defined the city's geography. The east side was originally written on the plat as "St. Anthony Falls" by William R. Marshall. It was simplified by Franklin Steele to "St. Anthony." As the city expanded, the east side and west side division of Minneapolis persisted. Old St. Anthony, Northeast and Southeast Minneapolis clung to the east side, since it conveyed the importance of the east bank of the city. Urban renewal in the late '50s divided north, northeast, south, southeast and southwest into a semblance of the present-day neighborhoods.

Before the parsing of the city into smaller and smaller distinct neighborhoods, there was a sense of community for many residents. One example was Frank Rog, the star athlete son of Polish immigrants and, later, mayor of Roseville, Minnesota. In his self-published memoir, *Let Me Be Frank*, he said, "My neighborhood was as diverse as they came. Russian, Polish, Irish, Syrian, Norwegian, Lebanese, Jewish...you name it, we had it. Most who lived in Lower Northeast were very poor, as they were new immigrants and had little education, but they were all willing to work if a job could be found." In Rog's youth, the "East Side" was his neighborhood. After urban renewal, his neighborhood was called St. Anthony West.

Minneapolis is composed of eleven communities—for example, Near North, Powderhorn, Longfellow, Phillips and University. Communities range from four to thirteen neighborhoods. The University community includes Cedar-Riverside, Como, Marcy-Holmes, Nicollet Island/East Bank, Prospect Park and University. Minneapolis neighborhoods defined by municipal government stand in stark contrast to those whimsically popularized "unofficial districts." These neighborhoods comprise more than one neighborhood, such as the Warehouse District, Old St. Anthony, Eat Street and Uptown. Old St. Anthony encompasses Marcy-Holmes and Nicollet Island/East Bank.

South Uptown was formerly CARAG (Calhoun Area Residents' Action Group), the southern portion of Uptown. However, Lake Calhoun's name was changed to one of the Dakota names for the lake, Bde Maka Ska, which translates to "Lake White Earth" or "Lake White Bank." In 2018, after nearly two hundred years, the neighborhood solicited a name change: South Uptown was decided. Neighborhoods considered part of Uptown include Lowry Hill East (the Wedge) and East Isles, while East Calhoun Community Organization (ECCO) is another neighborhood that is in the process of changing its name.

In 1929, the original Lagoon Theatre was renamed the Uptown; the name slowly took hold for the surrounding neighborhood while the marquee shined. But before Uptown, the vicinity of Lake of the Isles and Bde Maka Ska had the longest European American and Native American interaction outside of Fort Snelling.

Near Bde Maka Ska, European Americans and Dakota settled and cooperated in the establishment of Eatonville—named after Andrew Jackson's secretary of war, John H. Eaton. With his ceremonial rank as major, Lawrence Taliaferro, a native Virginian Indian agent of Italian patrician background, sponsored the village. Taliaferro also was a friend of President James Monroe and likewise a slaveholder. He taught agriculture to Cloud Man, or Mahpiyawicasta, and the Mdewakanton Dakota because the fur trade was depleted. Together they achieved agricultural success in the project Taliaferro called his "Lake Harriet Experiment." Men also worked the land, then traditionally a woman's job. In 1831, there were three hundred people in the summer village. Then settlement pushed Native Americans farther west. The Mdewakanton were in drawn into territorial conflict with the Ojibwe, and in the 1840s they abandoned their summer village.

Prospect Park.

A contemporary of that period, Charlotte O. Van Cleve reminisced about her childhood as the daughter of a soldier stationed at Fort Snelling, in *Three Score Years and Ten* (1888). She wrote, "How sweet those berries were, and how delicious the fish which we caught in the pretty Lakes Calhoun and Harriet, the one named for the great statesman, the other for Mrs. Leavenworth." The beauty of the Lake District—both lakes and hills—were a byproduct of glaciation that was appreciated by both the Native Americans and the European settlers, for a time. However, the two parties' opinions differed on the path of development and the future of the lake now called Bde Maka Ska.

In 1834, Gideon and Samuel Pond of Connecticut arrived as lay missionaries. Their cabin was the first European American permanent structure in the future Minneapolis. On the present-day site of St. Mary's Greek Orthodox Church for more than five decades, it was annexed by the city. The brothers, both "born again in Christ," were products of the Second Great Awakening. They journeyed to St. Louis and Galena, Illinois, before arriving at Fort Snelling. There they learned and studied the Dakota language and wrote books on the topic. Mary Lethert Wingerd wrote of the Ponds in *North Country*, "Agent Taliaferro must have recognized the exceptional character of the brothers. He entrusted them to establish a mission at his prized agricultural experiment, located near the village of Cloud Man, on Lake Calhoun [Bde Maka Ska]." The Ponds nurtured relationships by learning the Dakota language, but the arrival of Reverend Jedediah Stevens weakened relations. Stevens espoused the standard racist claptrap of those days, and both the tribe and Ponds were condescended to and alienated by the reverend. In 1842, Samuel and Gideon established Oak Grove in present-day Bloomington. Later, Samuel moved down river to Chief Shakopee, and a village that later became the city of the same name.

Samuel Pond said of the Dakota's character in *The Dakota or Sioux in Minnesota as They Were in 1834*, "Industry and enterprise were nowhere more highly prized than among Dakotas, and a lazy man or woman was regarded as a public nuisance, for if one did not work others work the harder. It is natural that white men who know little about the Dakotas, when they see many of them unwilling to engage in agricultural labors, should regard them as lazy, good-for-nothing fellows." He also commented on their form of government, "The government of the Dakotas was purely democratic, the people holding all the powers of government in their own hands, and never delegating them to others except temporarily and for special purposes." Moreover, he observed decision-making without violence and women were treated as near equals.

In 1849, Charles Mosseaux (variously rendered as Mousseau, or even Musou, by John Stevens), the French voyageur of the American Fur Company, staked first claim east of Lake Calhoun, now Bde Maka Ska.

Later in the nineteenth century, a resort area was concentrated on the shores of Bde Maka Ska. One of the grandest was to be Louis Menage's Lake Side Park. It was planned on 130 acres on the present-day site of the Minikahda Club capped with an 80-foot-tall observatory. This scheme failed. Menage had relocated from New York, and typically, as David A. Lanegran and Ernest R. Sandeen wrote in *The Lake District*, "Menage had lung problems and, like many other people from the East and South during that era, was lured to Minnesota by the exaggerated claims made about the state's invigorating climate."

A steam-powered motor line—the Minneapolis, Lyndale and Minnetonka—transported tourists from Nicollet Avenue to 31st Street to Bde Maka Ska and summer hotels along the shore in 1879. In 1883, Menage's luxury hotel, the Lyndale, opened. It was destroyed by a fire in 1888. The resort closed. Menage continued developing real estate throughout the city in Prospect Park, Windom Park, Bloomington Avenue and "cottage city," the former name for the once modest homes on the southern edge of Bde Maka Ska.

Roswell P. Russell was another early settler in the heart of present-day Uptown. He first settled in St. Anthony. He later staked a claim centered on 28th Street and Hennepin Avenue. Decades later, his mansion was leveled and the property occupied by West High from 1908 to 1982.

Lowry Hill was first known as the Devil's Backbone before residential development softened its appearance. Later, the neighborhood was one of the toniest sections of town and lined with the mansions of Minneapolis's late nineteenth-century elites. In 1880, the nearby Kenwood neighborhood was platted, an upper-class streetcar suburb. Lowry Hill's boundaries range from the Walker Art Center to 22nd Street to Kennilworth Parkway to Hennepin Avenue. After Calvin C. Goodrich of Ohio sold 50 percent interest in the land to his son-in-law, Thomas Lowry, originally from Illinois, the Groveland Addition was developed. In 1867, Lowry arrived to practice law and sell real estate. He constructed a French Second Empire mansion at Hennepin Avenue and Groveland Terrace that was razed during the Depression.

For decades outside the city limit, the Camden neighborhood was organized separately from the city. First, it was agricultural farmsteads and then sawmills and assorted industry. Charles Farrington and Elijah Austin made the first claims in North Minneapolis. Early settlers included Rufus Farnham Jr. and Sr. They had voted for the prohibition of intoxicating beverages in St. Anthony that was ruled unconstitutional. In 1853, they relocated and built a shingle mill at the creek in the area, later known as Camden. In that year, David Morgan constructed a flour mill. John Ware Dow also constructed a log house at present-day 44th and Humboldt Avenue N. John Bohanon arrived from Maine and lost a claim at 5th Street and Hennepin Avenue S—the future site of the West Hotel. His claim was 160 acres in North Minneapolis at Humboldt Avenue North and 40th to 44th Avenues in Camden.

The Powderhorn community is centered on the eponymously named park. In 1887, the neighborhood was annexed as part of the city of Minneapolis. The Minneapolis Park Board acquired Powderhorn Lake Park in 1890. It then was twenty-five acres and cost $40,000. Eventually, the park encompassed sixty-five and a half acres. Swampland dominated the park, so the park board improved the land with the dredging of Powderhorn Lake. In 1925, the south side of the lake was filled in, and the powderhorn shape was lost. The annual In the Heart of the Beast Mask Theatre's May Day Festival has been hosted by the neighborhood for over forty-five years.

The Longfellow community is a large residential area in South Minneapolis. It is located between Hiawatha Avenue, the Mississippi River and Midtown Greenway on the north and Minnehaha Park in the south. Since the 1960s, Longfellow has been the community name given by local government. The community was named after Henry Wadsworth Longfellow, who wrote the epic poem *The Song of Hiawatha* in 1855. He used largely fabricated Ojibwe and Dakota legends, and the poem tells the story of the warrior Hiawatha falling in love with Minnehaha. In the 1930s, the area was known as "southtown."

Speculators and farmers first settled in the future Longfellow neighborhood. In 1853, there was a land sale and surveying of the area. Minnehaha Creek was then Brown's Creek, and Ard Godfrey had a claim and a mill near the falls. The falls were first known as Little Falls and, later, Brown's Falls. The name was likely to honor Major General Jacob Brown, but a few historians also posited Joseph R. Brown. Historian Edward D. Neill contended the falls were named after Major General Jacob Brown.

Minnehaha Falls has a fifty-three-foot drop. Since 1823, travelers have visited the falls as a scenic attraction. Charlotte Van Cleve traveled as a child

Downtown Minneapolis from Farview Park.

Ard Godfrey House.

The Parkway Theater in the McRae Park neighborhood.

from Fort Snelling to "Little Falls." She wrote: "The picture in my mind of this gem of beauty, makes the sheet of water wider and more circular than it is now, I know it was fresher and newer, and there was no saloon there then, no fence, no tables and benches, cut up and disfigured with names and nonsense, no noisy railroad, no hotel, it was just our dear pure 'Little Falls' with its graceful ferns, its bright flowers, its bird music and its lovely water-fall." The *Minnesota Handbook* said, "Minnehaha Falls…[was] probably the most romantic and beautiful cascade in the Union." In 1885, Minnehaha was designated as a park. Prominent authors and politicians such as Henry David Thoreau, Mark Twain and Lyndon Baines Johnson have visited the falls.

In 1857, Falls City was laid out in the vicinity north of Minnehaha Falls. The borders followed the Mississippi River north to near present-day 24th Street west to 38th Avenue and after Lake Street northwest to roughly 33rd Avenue. Five businessmen platted six hundred lots, but then the Panic of 1857 occurred only a few lots were sold. In 1863 and 1866, the two largest investors relocated, and the only evidence that remains is a few blocks in the Seward neighborhood.

The Ford Bridge (Inter City Bridge) was constructed between 1925 and 1927. The bridge designed by Norwegian immigrant Frederick Cappelen (1857–1921) connected Longfellow and South Minneapolis with the Highland Park neighborhood and St. Paul.

The Michael J. Dowling School for Crippled Children was built on the Mississippi River to the north of where the future bridge was built. In 1920, the progressive school for children with disabilities was the second school of its kind in Minneapolis. The school board moved the disabilities school from a church building on 18th and Dupont Avenues in North Minneapolis.

Dowling was a banker and educator. He also had a lifelong disability. Caught in a blizzard as a twelve-year-old, he lost both legs below the knees, most fingers on the right hand and the left hand below the elbow to frostbite. His limbs were partially amputated. William Eustis donated twenty-one acres for the Dowling School west of the West River Parkway. Unable to walk as a boy, the former mayor of Minneapolis empathized with young people with special needs.

President Franklin Delano Roosevelt dedicated the pool at Dowling on October 9, 1936. The pool was constructed by the WPA (Works Progress Administration), an important New Deal program. The *Minneapolis Tribune* wrote on October 10, "President Sees Pool, Talks to Children at

Dowling Pool." FDR had spent five hours in the Twin Cities and traveled to Minneapolis after his train arrived in St. Paul. For the ceremony, there were five thousand attendees, with fifteen-year-old student Martin Croze in his wheelchair making a brief address. His mother organized the pool campaign. FDR had visited a similar school in Warm Springs, Georgia. In his address, FDR hinted at his disability, the *Tribune* reported, "I hope that all of you will be able to learn to swim in this fine pool. Swimming, you know, is the only exercise I can take." In 1987, the school was reorganized as an Urban Environmental Learning Center.

Robert "Fish" Jones established the infamous zoo in the Longfellow neighborhood near Minnehaha Falls. Jones was a small man smartly attired in a silk high hat, a gold-headed cane and a Vandyke beard. He was a purveyor of fish and seafood. His first zoo was at the present-day Basilica site. The zoo and aviary enraged the locals with ferocious noise and unsightliness. So, to the chagrin of the Minneapolis Park Board, Jones purchased property near Minnehaha Falls from two heirs of Franklin Steele.

He relocated to Longfellow Gardens (1907–34). The gardens were easily accessible by streetcars or trains, and the zoo included lions, bears, camels, elephants, Tasmanian devils and many more animals. But as the

Jacob Fjelde's statue of Minnehaha and Hiawatha.

Princess Depot.

Stone Arch Festival with historic Mill District in background.

zoo expanded, the neighbors complained about the sounds and smells. In 1922, the park board petitioned to acquire the creek property. The zoo was condemned by the city in the 1920s but didn't close until his death in 1930.

During the 1930s, the Minneapolis Planning Commission combined the Longfellow and the Seward neighborhoods. But in 1983, Longfellow was split from Seward. Longfellow also became a Minneapolis community that included the Seward neighborhood.

Since the 1960s, Seward developed a reputation as a progressive and hippie community. The expansion on the West Bank of the University of Minnesota precipitated tenants and homeowners settling in the neighborhood.

Milwaukee Avenue is an essential story in Seward's history. The thoroughfare was originally an alley, and the homes were workingmen's cottages, some constructed with brick. *Milwaukee Avenue* says, regarding urban renewal, "Several goals emerged: attracting middle-class families and businesses back into the city, rebuilding slum areas, improving the quality of life, improving tax revenues and improving the real estate market."

Urban renewal confronted Minneapolis communities and neighborhoods after World War II. First, there was urban flight to the suburbs, followed in the succeeding decades by interstate highways I-94 and I-35W cutting through the city.

YOUR GUIDE TO HISTORY

Ard Godfrey House/Chute Square
28 University Avenue SE
Minneapolis, MN 55414
(612) 813-5300
www.womansclub.org
Prices vary—reservations required except for special events

The Ard Godfrey House is the oldest surviving frame house in Minneapolis. The former home of the first postmaster of old St. Anthony, it was originally built at Main Street and 2nd Avenue SE in 1848. The house was moved several times before arriving in Chute Square Park in 1907. It opens only for special events and private tours.

Longfellow Gardens

3933 East Minnehaha Parkway
Minneapolis, MN 55417
(612) 230-6400
www.minneapolisparks.org
Free to the public

Longfellow Gardens, with its winding walking paths and incredible displays of both native and exotic plants and flowers, is the former site of the Longfellow Zoological Gardens, owned and operated by Robert "Fish" Jones from 1907 to 1923. He named his attraction after Henry Wadsworth Longfellow. *Hiawatha and Minnehaha* was sculpted by Jacob Fjelde near the falls. After appearing at the World's Columbian Exchange in Chicago in 1893, the sculpture was relocated to the present site nearly two decades later, in 1912.

Princess Depot

4900 S Minnehaha Drive
Minneapolis, MN 55417
(612) 230-6400
www.minneapolisparks.org
Free

The Princess Depot (1877) was a former bustling rail stop for day trippers and vacationers visiting Minnehaha Falls. In the depot's pre–World War I heyday, three trains made thirteen round trips daily. After decommissioning the stop in 1963, the Milwaukee Road Railroad gave the depot to the Minnesota Historical Society. The Minnesota Transportation Museum converted the little depot into a free museum.

Neighborhood Festivals

Art-A-Whirl

2205 California Street NE, Suite 118
Minneapolis, MN
(612) 788-1679
nemaa.org

Since 1996, Art-A-Whirl has showcased open art studio tours throughout Northeast Minneapolis neighborhoods. Organized by the nonprofit Northeast Minneapolis Arts Association (NEMAA), the three-day event regularly draws forty thousand visitors.

Celebrate Northeast Parade

2329 Central Avenue NE
Minneapolis, MN 55418
(612) 378-0050
www.mplschamber.com/programming/parade

Every June since 1929, Northeast Minneapolis residents host Celebrate Northeast Parade, which features marching bands, community royalty and local politicians. It's one of the largest community parades in the state of Minnesota and is the second-longest running. Check site for exact date and start time.

Fourth of July Events

www.minneapolis.org/calendar/holidays/july-4th/

Any event in summer brings out the best in a city like Minneapolis. There are free fireworks on the Mississippi River, best viewed on Nicollet Island and Old Saint Anthony and from the highest point of Gold Medal Park.

In the Heart of the Beast MayDay Celebration

(612) 540-5385
hobt.org/mayday

Every spring, Heart of the Beast puts on its spectacular MayDay Parade (held on the first Sunday of May), with musical performances, trick bicyclists and unicyclists, gigantic puppets, dancers and lots and lots of costumes, with the parade route following Bloomington Avenue S from 25th Street E and ending in a big celebration at Powderhorn Park. Each year has a different theme, usually based on a social or environmental issue.

Unfortunately, the future of the event is uncertain due to financing issues.

Northeast Dog Parade

heartofnortheast.com
The end of July—check website for meeting place and official date

The Northeast Dog Parade is exactly what it sounds like—it's a parade of dogs and their owners culminating in a big party at the riverfront, where dogs complete for prizes in costume and skill contests. You don't have to have a dog to enjoy the summer spectacle of hundreds of dogs enjoying a nice, summer day.

Northern Spark Festival

northernspark.org

The Northern Spark Festival is an all-night festival that takes place throughout Minneapolis (mostly downtown and the U of M campus area). Light shows, temporary sculpture installations, calliope pizza ovens, opportunities to make homemade books with an antique letterpress and demonstrations showcasing the skills of nocturnal birds of prey are just a few of the events that have made attending previous festivals worth staying up late at night.

Stone Arch Festival

Old Saint Anthony Main Street and Father Hennepin Bluff Park
www.stonearchbridgefestival.com
Father's Day weekend

The Stone Arch Festival unofficially kicks off Minneapolis's summer, with live musical performances, family and kids' dance stages, hundreds of local artists' kiosks, an antique car show and lots of food and summer treats.

4

MILL CITY

MINNEAPOLIS INDUSTRIAL DEVELOPMENT

Minneapolis attracted capital, settlers and labor to the Mill City. Moreover, the seemingly endless potential of the Falls of St. Anthony provided energy for the burgeoning milling industry. Milling dominated St. Anthony and Minneapolis, first, lumber milling and the great white pines of the Rum River and to the north. Then flour emerged and truly elevated Minneapolis's economy in the old Northwest and, later, Upper Midwest. As the flour milling developed, two families consolidated the industry and eventually dominated local flour milling as well as Minneapolis and state politics—the Pillsbury and Washburn families.

Tragedy affected the flour milling industry and was the impetus for innovation that led to consolidation. On May 2, 1878, the Washburn A Mill explosion killed eighteen, and seven mills were destroyed. The blast was heard in St. Paul. In the aftermath, University of Minnesota physicist Louis W. Peck and chemist Stephen F. Peckham studied the disaster, and the professors concluded millstone dust sparked and ignited the fire. In "History of Hennepin County," Reverend Edward D. Neill described the disaster: "a terrific explosion took place in the Washburn 'A' Mill, which shook the solid land like an earthquake, breaking thousands of dollars' worth of glass in the city, and felt distinctly at St. Paul, ten miles away." The *Minneapolis Tribune* reported, "Minneapolis has with a calamity the suddenness and horror of which it is difficult for the mind to conceive. For the twinkling of an eye, by an explosion that shook the city like the rocking of an earthquake, the largest, highest, and probably the heaviest stone structure in Minneapolis,"

View of the Mill City Museum from the Mill Ruins Park.

Grain Belt Beer sign.

the Washburn A Mill, was "leveled." The paper reported three mills were lost, and "two planing mills, two machine shops, a lumberyard, and several cooper shops and other buildings, a record of which will be found elsewhere, joined the procession of flame, and considering the boisterous wind prevailing, and the combustible material in its path, the workers is the whole lower portion of the city escaped the fate which it was threatened." There were fourteen headlines in the style of the day, including "Five Flouring Mills and Other Valuable Buildings Scattered in Countless Fragments." Newspapers did not agree on the number of mills destroyed. But the disaster was "the most direful calamity which has ever befallen the city of Minneapolis."

Charles Pillsbury, suddenly and meteorically, emerged. One of the two major millers in Minneapolis, he purchased the foreclosed Alaska or Taylor Bros. Mill in 1870. In part, his success was sparked by taking advantage of circumstances after the Panic of 1873. Money was tight, but Pillsbury was able to purchase an older east side mill in 1874. As John Anfinson wrote, "By 1874 Charles A. Pillsbury and Company owned five mills, and in 1879 Washburn-Crosby Company owned three. Together, the two companies produced more than half the city's flour."

Historic Pillsbury Mill complex, transformed into condos.

In 1875, Pillsbury quit the hardware business, first on Main Street in Lower Town St. Anthony, and later in Bridge Square, for milling. From there, Pillsbury figured out the modern milling practices used by the Washburn and Company and then received national—and even international attention—with Pillsbury's "best" flour. In 1880, the Pillsbury A Mill was constructed by Le Roy S. Buffington (1847–1931). He designed the seven-story mill that doubled the production of the Washburn A Mill. In 1883, when the Pillsbury A Mill was completed, Minneapolis's flour milling production increased from 15,200 to 20,400 barrels daily.

In 1880, twenty-seven Minneapolis mills produced two million barrels of flour a year. Between 1880 and 1930, Minneapolis was the nation's largest flour producer. As Kane said in *The Falls of St. Anthony*, "In 1880, unable to keep pace with the northern giant, St. Louis yielded its crown—a crown Minneapolis was to wear for fifty years."

Sawmilling flourished early in Minneapolis because of the vast white pine forest from the Rum River to the north. And the names involved in lumber milling—Walker, Washburn and others—produced greater than 200 million board feet in 1875. However, sawmilling changed the next year, when C.C.

and W.D. Washburn closed six sawmills on the west side. Sawmilling was not as lucrative as flour milling.

By the 1880s, steam power was readily available and affordable. Lumber mills moved upriver, where logs could be transported or floated down the Mississippi River but north of the water power and to North Minneapolis.

In *Archeology of the Central Minneapolis Riverfront, Part II*, Scott F. Anfinson, the former state archaeologist, wrote, "The city of Minneapolis is where it is because of the waterpower potentials of St. Anthony Falls."

Flour milling became the monolithic industry on the west side because the industry yielded the largest profits. In the 1870s, milling technology advanced with "new process flour." But there were several baby steps that preceded the technological leap forward. The first turbines were used in the 1840s. They replaced water wheels in the 1850s and 1860s. The V-shaped dam was constructed to force water to both the east and west banks for development of waterpower in 1857.

Other innovations included the gradual reduction process: steel rollers replaced millstones. The Berhns Millstone Exhaust System limited flour dust and prevented explosions and fires. These innovations transformed Minneapolis into the "Budapest of North America."

In 1870, C.C. Washburn hired Alabama native George H. Christian. He visited Hungary and brought back the "middlings purifier." With this new technology, hard spring wheat that grew in the region was made marketable—even more desirable. The hard and dark layer of bran was sorted out and did not discolor or darken the flour. It was white—the ultimate triumph of industrial processing. Borchert described the process: "In the early 1870s, Minneapolis millers adopted a technique, developed in Dundas, Minnesota, that made drastic improvements in the quality of the flour. This process involved separating the husk and bran from the flour with a series of sieves and blowers a middlings purifier."

Milling innovations resulted in the trade expanding nationally and internationally. In 1877, silent partner William H. Dunwoody negotiated a trade deal for nearly a year in England to sell flour for the Washburn-Crosby Company. Thereafter, General Mills elevated the companies' reputation on the world stage. Financial earnings proved their status. Dunwoody was both a mover and shaker in business as well as in local philanthropy. The Dunwoody College of Technology is named in his honor. The private not-for-profit trade school has served the community since the year of his death, 1914.

In 1890, four corporations controlled 87 percent of Minneapolis's milling capacity. Three corporations produced 97 percent of the west side flour. However, flour milling expanded nationally and even globally with consolidation. Furthermore, flour milling corporations reshuffled organization in response to federal policy. Following the passage of the Dingley Tariff (1897), wheat imported from Canada was shipped back as flour "duty free," which benefited milling rivals in the East, as did the rates paid for freight.

Pillsbury-Washburn Flour Mills Co. Ltd. (London financial syndicate) existed from 1889 to 1908, the largest flour company in the world. In 1893, Charles Bovey promoted the export of Gold Medal Flour. But in 1908, the company went into receivership, and the two largest milling companies in Minneapolis were split apart.

After 1930, flour production steadily diminished in Minneapolis. In 1928, General Mills was organized and expanded into markets across the United States, beginning with Wichita Falls, Texas. In 1931, Buffalo, New York, led the nation in flour production. It surpassed Minneapolis because of the decentralization of flour milling. Shipping rates favored eastern mills and tariffs. The impact was swiftly and heavily felt by Minneapolis mills—the Zenith, Pettit, Galaxy, Pillsbury B, Washburn B, Northwestern and North Star Feed Mill all closed by 1932.

Pillsbury sign.

Over the next thirty-plus years, many Minneapolis flour mills were abandoned. In 1965, the last mill on the west side, the Washburn-Crosby A Mill, closed. On the east side, the Pillsbury A Mill remained the only operating mill. Archer Daniels Midland (ADM), with headquarters in Chicago, purchased the mill in 1992. It permanently closed in 2003.

Nina Archabal was the Minnesota Historical Society director from 1987 to 2011. She recalled the riverfront in MRROHP, "My memory of that place is of an incredibly cold, abandoned place where nothing was happening, but where, clearly, something *had* happened that was really big, but it was all gone." The experience was an early memory of Minneapolis. As director, she served a pivotal role in the Minneapolis riverfront redevelopment.

In 2001, General Mills acquired Pillsbury from Diageo, and the companies merged again.

Minneapolis's economy flourished because of business diversification. The success of milling fueled banking, railroads, warehousing, land development and real estate businesses. These businesses assisted flour milling and the relentless growth of the industry in the late nineteenth century. Many investors in these enterprises arrived from the milling industry with extra earnings, looking for investment possibilities. Others were attracted from far-flung locales to prosper by Minneapolis's expanding economy.

In the 1880s, Minneapolis experienced the greatest growth in physical size and population. The population tripled from 46,887 in 1880 to 129,000 in 1885. Through 1890, the dramatic demographic growth continued, and the population numbers reached 164,738. The outcome of explosive population numbers necessitated the new scale of business that grew along with diversification. The geographic area of the city also tripled, and thirteen thousand new buildings were constructed. Brick and stone structures replaced the pioneer's wood buildings.

Allied businesses emerged, as Wells noted: "Between 1878 and 1883, on the river of wheat and timber that flowed into the milling district, Minneapolis emerged as the center of regional manufacturing." Minneapolis became the jobbing center of the Upper Midwest, which led to the development of its vast warehouse district, especially after 1880. Jobbing involved the shipping of bales, boxes and barrels. In addition, cooperages made packaging for the factories.

In the 1880s, the most railroad track in the state was laid in Minneapolis. This allowed for allied industries to cluster along train tracks. With better transportation, and access along train routes to more markets, these businesses experienced unprecedented growth.

Grain Exchange Building.

Brewing dovetailed with Minneapolis's industrial growth. The beer industry began almost with settlement in St. Anthony, but it was opposed by many New England prohibitionists. They also often espoused xenophobic opinions about German immigrants who owned and were employed in the majority of Minneapolis breweries. Breweries were established in the German sections of the city, such as Northeast, Bohemian Flats and North Minneapolis, with a few ephemeral breweries in South Minneapolis.

Minneapolis Brewing Company, and later, Grain Belt Brewing, commenced when John Orth emigrated from Alsace, then under French rule. With his German cultural heritage, he began operations with his wife, Mary, in St. Anthony as Orth Brewing in 1848. After Anthony Yoerg in St. Paul in 1848, he was the second brewer in the state. Both men arrived as the lager revolution began to influence beer drinkers' expectations. Lager beer

Former Grain Belt Beer brewery.

has bottom-sinking yeast in the fermentation and is cold "lagered" or stored. John Wagner introduced the first lager yeast in Philadelphia. In 1840, he arrived in the United States from the German state of Bavaria. The cleaner, lighter-hued beer took off. And since then, cheaply mass-produced corporate lagers have dominated American markets—even today, with the emergence of distinctive craft beers.

Orth's original brewery was a cozy eighteen by thirty feet with water from artesian wells. The first brewery in Hennepin County was at the locally famous site (1215 Marshall Street). Orth's initial beer styles included ales, porters and lagers. On Nicollet Island, caves with sandstone foundations were used to store and age beer.

In 1890, four Minneapolis breweries organized as the Minneapolis Brewing Company: Orth, Heinrich, Germania and Noerenberg. Gluek Brewing was also sought in the consolidation, but the company was successful enough to decline. A new brewery was constructed with a capacity of 150,000 barrels and was nearly destroyed by fire in 1893. The new company's flagship, Golden Grain Belt beer, received countless accolades and became the brewery's name. Lager beer has low alcohol content compared to hard liquor, and it was promoted for public health. In 1915, Grain Belt Brewing was incorporated in Nebraska. This decision signaled Grain Belt's position as a budding national brand.

Before Prohibition, breweries could both produce beer and own bars, referred to as tied saloons. Vertical integration of the brewing industry was unregulated. Breweries were permitted to brew, distribute and own saloons that exclusively sold their beer. The *Minneapolis Journal* reported that in 1908, only 38 of 432 bars in Minneapolis had individual owner and were not brewery owned. Breweries owned an astonishing amount of city property. The number of saloons owned included: Minneapolis Brewing Company, 131; Gluek, 86; Purity, 38; and Milwaukee's Blatz, 41. Doug Hoverson said in *Land of Amber Waters*, "The concentration of brewery-owned saloons in the Twin Cities was higher than almost any other major American city." Northeast Minneapolis, in particular, the first ward, had the largest concentration of breweries. In the first ward, Northeast breweries owned 132 lots.

After two years, Gottlieb Gluek moved on from John Orth Brewing. In 1857, Gluek founded a brewery about a mile north (at Marshall Street and 20th Avenue NE). He partnered with John Rank as the Mississippi Brewery. In 1862, Gluek assumed sole ownership, and the brewery production dramatically increased in the 1870s. But in 1880, a fire damaged the brewery. Gottlieb died, and his sons—Louis, Charles and John—took the helm. In 1893, the brewery was incorporated as Gluek's Brewing. After Prohibition, despite the number of tied saloons in Minneapolis, the brewery's beer distribution was uncompetitive out of state with Grain Belt Brewing. The Glueks succeeded with beers such as Pilsener Pale and Bock. Later, Gluek distributed a famous—or infamous depending on taste— malt liquor, nicknamed "Green Death" for the headaches it induced. The beer was patented as "stite." But Gluek was too small a brewer with the emergence of dominant national brewers and consolidation. The brewery was sold to G. Heileman in 1964. The brewery closed, and it was demolished in 1966.

Following the Civil War, there was also a brewing boom at the "Brewery Flats" in Minneapolis. In 1866, John Kranzlein and John Mueller brewed beer as Minneapolis Brewery. The brewery lasted about a year before undergoing a rapid change of ownership. Eventually acquired by John Heinrich, it was known as Heinrich Brewing. At the south end of the Mississippi River bluffs in the lower levee of the Bohemian Flats (present-day West River Parkway, 4th Street S and the Mississippi River), the area was known as the Brewery Flats because of the eighty-foot-high limestone and sandstone cliffs. It was not until the mid-1880s that the north end of the flats was populated by poor immigrants and became more commonly known as the Bohemian Flats.

F.D. Noerenberg had a similar history at the north end of the flats (20th Avenue S and Bluff Street). The brewery began as Anton Zahler Brewing (1874–77) and also City Brewery. Zahler partnered with Noerenberg, who took control entirely from 1880 to the 1890. In the merger, the breweries became part of Minneapolis Brewing. About1900, the river flat breweries were torn down and replaced by barge terminal and coal storage. Germania Brewing also joined the merger. Before, it had been a succession of breweries around Keegan Lake—later known as Wirth Lake.

Besides larger brewers, Minneapolis had numerous small breweries come and go. Some remained in business only a year or more, for example, the Scandinavian-named Olson and Johnson Brewing that sold low-alcohol *weiss* beer in Northeast Minneapolis around 1877. Other breweries served a niche market like Hennepin Brewing, which specialized in low alcohol beers from 1910 to 1920.

Lauritzen Brewing sold beer that allegedly improved the imbibers' health. Dr. Peter Lauritzen operated the snake oil brewery from 1903 to 1909. It was a regimen of the Swedish Movement Cure Institute—health based on exercise and diet. The brewery recommended its beer to improve digestive health. But the beer also made drinkers drunk. The brewery moved to South Minneapolis.

In Minneapolis, newspapers ads appeared appealing to thirsty, beer-guzzling workers. Many breweries advertised to attract business for their beers. Breweries came and went, in ad space, too, like Christ C. Hohl of North Minneapolis, "Bottler of Ale & Porter," said in the June 22, 1867 *Minneapolis Tribune*. As time passed, the ads became more sophisticated, yet they included information contrary to modern scientific knowledge.

By 1904, the Gluek Brewing Company presented increasingly sophisticated advertising. A recurring ad in that year for the *Minneapolis Journal* read, "Gluek Brewing Co. Brewers and bottlers of high grade beers…" The same simple and concise ad ran for years until a more aggressive approach was used that included snake oil salesmanship.

In 1906, a repeating ad for Gluek's Pilsener was particularly curious. It led with the headline "A Healthy Food vs. a Nerve Stimulant" above an illustration of a prissy and refined bourgeois beer guzzler beside a stiff, haggard gentleman coffee drinker sitting at a table. The ad said, "You never see a dyspeptic beer drinker, but you see hundreds of people every day who drink coffee and tea, which plays havoc with their stomach. Beer is a food and few are more easily digested." It concluded, "Gluek's Pilsener is a mild, wholesome, refreshing beer. It will surely please you." And then, the sale—"Order a case for your home." The ad provided a phone number, of course, for delivery.

Ads were also planted in articles. One such ad for Grain Belt Beer was tucked into "American Railway Men Rescue London" in the *Minneapolis Journal* on June 27, 1903: "He is expected to succeed just as the man who first produced golden grain belt beer succeeded where generations of foreign brewers had failed. Perseverance and a determination to have this beer absolutely pure have made it what it is, the most healthful and refreshing beer ever brewed." The article/ad concluded, "Try a case at home; it's good for all the family."

Like beer brewing, the railroad demonstrated Minneapolis cultural industrialization and advancement as a city. Both were industrial products; while beer provided leisure and pleasure, the railroad was truly transformative. In 1883, the speed of the railroad necessitated "railroad time."

In 1853, the St. Paul, St. Anthony Railroad was chartered. On June 28, 1862, the *William Crooks* was the first train for the St. Paul and Pacific Railroad between the "Capitol City" and St. Anthony. In the anthology *North Star State*, Richard Francaviglia asserted, "A new era began in Minnesota in 1862 when the state's first train made its initial run between St. Paul and St. Anthony."

The *William Crooks*, an American Standard locomotive, traveled approximately ten miles from Phalen Creek to just south of St. Anthony. The arrival of railroads transformed Minneapolis's industrial development. As Borchert said in *The Legacy of Minneapolis*, "The large eastern manufacturers were able to sell their goods in Minneapolis at the same price as locally produced goods. As a result, many factories in Minneapolis were forced out of business. The early ironworks, woolen mills, and paper mills were replaced by flour mills." One example of this process of profitability was at the Lee and Hardenburgh Ironworks (1865). In 1879, it was demolished to make room for the colossal Crown Roller Mill (1880), the second-largest west side mill.

In 1883, the Minneapolis, Sault Ste. Marie and Atlantic commenced— after consolidation, the railroad became the Soo Line. The Soo Line liberated Minneapolis millers and St. Paul shippers, who could bypass inflated shipping rates in Chicago.

The Minneapolis Industrial Exposition, like the railroad, proved the city. The industrial exposition demonstrated not only the state's regional achievements but also placed Minneapolis on the national stage. The gargantuan structure would host the 1892 Republican Convention.

Civic fundraising was necessary for such a mammoth endeavor. Private subscriptions raised $250,000 for the colossal exhibition hall. When the building opened, the *Minneapolis Tribune* credited the paper with proposing the exposition space and inspiring local businessmen to espouse the lofty dream.

Isaac Hodgson designed the Minneapolis Industrial Exposition Building; it was constructed of Mankato stone and bricks and boasted a 240-foot corner tower. On Main Street, the building stood 356 feet high, with the highest point 600 feet high on Bank Street. In total, the building occupied approximately 5.5 acres.

The exposition hall opened to the greatest hoopla then seen in the city's history on September 11, 1886. The newspaper headlines and accompanying stories spoke to the event's importance. The industrial exposition's grand opening received twelve page-one headlines.

The gala opening night celebration occurred on August 23, 1886. The *Tribune* reported the next day, "A few minutes after 2 o'clock Grand Marshall D.M. Gillmore formed the procession at the West Hotel. The glittering and stately military men, grave and reverend judges of the courts, sedate city fathers of St. Paul and Minneapolis, the proud and gratified directors reinforcing the blue badged stockholders, ex-governors and distinguished guests, fell obediently in line and reached the building by the suspension bridge amid crowds which taxed the capacity of the streets to the utmost."

The audience was first addressed by William D. Washburn. Then Mayor "Doc" Ames gave a "short and felicitous speech of Welcome," said the *Tribune*.

A telegram of congratulations was sent by First Lady Frances Cleveland. She pushed an "electric button" that started "machinery" that traveled to the exposition. The telegraph message was sent to the president of the exposition. As the *Tribune* described on August 24, 1886, "The circuit was open the whole distance, and within two minutes after Mrs. Cleveland had pressed the button the reply came from Minneapolis that the machinery was working beautifully." Within six years, the Republican National Convention was held at the Minneapolis Industrial Exposition.

In 1892, the Republican National Convention renominated Benjamin Harrison. He faced a weak challenge from James G. Blaine at the convention. However, Harrison would go on to lose to Grover Cleveland in the general election in the fall.

African Americans accounted for 13 percent of the delegates, numbering 116 at the convention. Frederick Douglass was a non-delegate participant at the Susan B. Anthony suffrage rally. Borchert summarized in "Legacy of Minneapolis," Minneapolis's emergence: "What better way to celebrate a city's position as the financial capital of a prosperous agricultural hinterland than to host the national convention for the Republican Party? That is exactly what Minneapolis did in 1892."

In 1893, the World's Columbian Exposition was the final blow for the Minneapolis Industrial Exposition. In that year, the exposition closed. Another factor was competition: expositions were held throughout the nation, including in St. Louis, Chicago, Cincinnati and Milwaukee.

The Mill City's rapid growth created the perfect storm for a natural calamity. The 1893 Fire or the East Side Fire exemplified Minneapolis's growing pains. The fire sparked on an industrialized Nicollet Island. Filled with lumber and wooden buildings, it was perfect kindling for an immense blaze and demonstrated the dangers of unregulated urban life.

Minneapolis, a budding metropolis, had triumphed in numerous ways. But more modern amenities were requisite, including a fire department. To meet the needs of the sprawling city, changes were necessary. Minneapolis was not alone—in fact, most major cities experienced conflagrations as part of the growing pains of civic responsibility. The Great Chicago Fire occurred in 1872, and conflagrations leveled sections of most major cities during this era. When the blaze burned down the east side in 1893, the Great Third Ward Fire in Milwaukee (October 28, 1892) was a recent memory.

Minneapolis's worst fire occurred on August 13, 1893. Total losses exceeded $1 million. The fire engulfed thirty city blocks, as Joseph Zalusky wrote in his article for *Hennepin County History* magazine.

On Nicollet Island, in the stables of the Cedar Lake Ice Company, the conflagration commenced. The fire leapt to Boom Island and destroyed numerous working-class homes. For a time, "it appeared…Northeast Minneapolis would be laid low and even the western bank was threatened, although the wind was blowing in the opposite direction." The fire destroyed 150 buildings before it was contained. But it could have been much worse, as the fire threatened to jump the river. After consuming Nicollet Island, it spread to Boom Island before heading north through Northeast Minneapolis to Broadway Avenue and the Minneapolis Brewing Company (Grain Belt Brewing). The "fireproof" construction saved the brewery, but losses totaled $117,000 and included the malt house, three bottling houses and more outbuildings, as well as damages to others. The Mississippi River flats burned from 6th to 15th Avenues NE. Zalusky, then the editor of the magazine, remembered the disaster in his youth as an eyewitness: "Your editor saw the smoke from this fire and ran all the way to Nicollet Island where, after viewing the fire, crossed over the East Channel of the Mississippi River by the way of the logs to get a clearer view (all kids skipped logs in the '90's). The fire was so hot here that the rails on the railroad right-of-way were twisted into all kinds of shapes by the heat."

The local newspapers reported on and sensationalized the tragic event. *Minneapolis Tribune* headlined "Fire Bugs at Work," a speculative stab that, no doubt, sold papers, but was never proven, on August 14, 1893. The fire, described as "the most extensive fire in the city's history," received an illustration and covered seven front-page columns. The reporters hypothesized on the source of the fire; not surprisingly, accusations were directed against the working poor.

But Northeast Minneapolis stuck together—the two-story Turner Hall, the then popular German American physical fitness organization, served as an ad hoc homeless shelter. Community members displaced by the fire gathered there. The *St. Paul Daily Globe* described the "East Side Fire," the day after the blaze on August 14, 1893. The headlines included: "A Column of Destruction," and "Flame-shot and Smoke-wrapped, It Eats Up with Fiery Breath over $1,000,000 Worth of Property." The headlines and reporting in St. Paul also became increasingly scandalous and sensationalistic: "Suspicion Entertained That There Was a Deliberately Planned Attempt to Create a Panic and Stampede." But the paper also described the scale of the conflagration: "The onward, irresistible rush of the terrible sea of flames was witnessed…by the residents of the thickly settled residence portion of the city, which seemed in the direct path of the fire fiend." The article continued, "All of the buildings on the south of the brewery were consumed, and the flames were carried to the west and around this immense structure."

The East Side Fire illustrated Minneapolis's shortcomings as a metropolis. In the aftermath, the city addressed the conflagration by reassessing the Minneapolis Fire Department, city ordinances and fire codes.

In contrast, Minneapolis constructed the first hydroelectric plant in the United States. The Falls of St. Anthony's energy resources lured lumber and flour millers to the east and west banks. Decades later, another use for the energy developed: hydroelectric power. Minneapolis innovated in milling, and later, on a smaller scale, in hydroelectric power.

In 1882, the Minnesota Brush Electric Company commenced hydroelectric energy production. The plant was completed before a similar project in Appleton, Wisconsin. As John Anfinson said in *Archeology of the Minneapolis Central Riverfront*, "Minneapolis was a pioneer in the development of electric power. One of the first central hydropower generating plants in the nation was built on Upton's Island at the foot of St. Anthony Falls in 1882." William D. Washburn, Joel B. Bassett, James Lovejoy, Sumner Farnham, Loren Fletcher, Charles M. Loring and Otis A. Pray financed the plant. John Anfinson elaborated in "12,000 Years at St. Anthony Falls": the Minnesota Brush Company "acquired land on Upton Island, built a small central power station, and installed five Brush arc-light generators with lines to businesses on Washington Avenue. On the evening of September 5, 1882, the company lit them with electricity generated by the first hydroelectric-power central station in the United States. By the end of 1885, 232 electric street lamps glowed in Minneapolis."

In 1895, William De La Barre commenced construction on the Lower Dam and hydro plant. Pillsbury-Washburn Company used the twenty-foot drop for the "Lower Dam." The project was completed in 1897. De La Barre arrived in Minneapolis in 1878, and he was employed by the Minneapolis Mill Company by 1883.

De La Barre sought to maximize the hydropower of the Falls of St. Anthony. He improved "Franklin Steele's original dam," as Anfinson wrote in "12,000 Years at St. Anthony Falls," by raising its height and extending the length of the tailraces, thereby raising the head, or distance the water fell, from eight feet to forty-five feet. It was called "De La Barre's Folly" when completed in 1897. However, De La Barre's engineering skills were lauded by Charles Pillsbury.

Pillsbury hired De La Barre to construct a hydroelectric plant on Hennepin Island. The Main Street Power Station was completed on the foundation of the former East Side sawmills at the St. Anthony Falls da, in 1908. Minneapolis General Electric Company provided the power for the Twin Cities Rapid Transit Company (TCRT). The plant was renovated in 1911 but ultimately closed in 1968. Later, the energy company merged as Northern States Power, and today, it is known as Xcel Energy.

The Mill City's hydroelectric power represented another success story. But nothing compared with flour milling. The powerbrokers' financial fortunes invested in a succession of mansion rows. First built on the edge of town, as time passed, palatial estates radiated out from downtown, with each generation moving farther away to avoid the incursion of hoi polloi.

In the early years of St. Anthony and Minneapolis, Nicollet Island was viewed as a lovely and retiring urban retreat for men of means. Colonel William King owned mansions on both Nicollet Island, an Italianate-style home on the present-day De La Salle High School site, and later near Lake Harriet. The lake was named after Fort Snelling commander Colonel Henry Leavenworth's wife. When private homes of the wealthy were on Nicollet

The old West Side Mill District.

Island, efforts were made to transform the island, in part, into a park. In 1857, early in the city's history, St. Peter boosters attempted to remove the capitol from St. Paul. Nicollet Island was a prospective site. Moreover, government buildings and swank housing were promised. This plan, like many others during the territorial days of the state, did not materialize. Nor did local elites stay on Nicollet Island, as industrialization and pollution clogged the riverfront.

During the late nineteenth and early twentieth centuries, Park Avenue concentrated the greatest mansion row. Clinton Morrison described the opulent street in *The Morrisons*: "The most stylish residential street in the city was Park Avenue, where the Crosbys, McKnights, Bells, Beckwiths, and Brooks, and later John Cowles, all lived." Morrison, of course, would take up residence in another mansion row, one centered on the William D. Washburn mansion—later Washburn Fair Oaks Park. It was surrounded by milling royalty: the Christians, Pillsburys and countless other homes. But on Park Avenue, the Swan Turnblad Mansion was the most massive and extravagant, but it was short-lived residential palatial estate.

YOUR GUIDE TO HISTORY

Bakken Museum
3537 Zenith Avenue S
Minneapolis, MN 55416
(612) 926-3878
thebakken.org
adults, $10; seniors and young adults 13–24, $8; children 4–12, $5

Medtronic co-founder Earl Bakken opened this museum in 1975. The Bakken Museum houses a variety of hands-on (and hands-off) science experiments involving electricity for visitors of all ages. Exhibits include a step-by-step instructional workshop on how patents for inventions are filed from beginning to end and models based on the history of electrical power use in Minneapolis.

Bde Maka Ska
3000 Calhoun Parkway
Minneapolis, MN 55408
(612) 230-6400
www.minneapolisparks.org

One of the primary reasons the park board was created in 1883 was to create parks at Bde Maka Ska (formerly Lake Calhoun) and neighboring Lake Harriet. Charles Loring, who would come to be known as the "Father of Minneapolis Parks," lobbied successfully for the new railway to bypass the north shore of Bde Maka Ska. When the Park Act was approved in 1883, architect Horace Cleveland was brought in to design the walkways and general layout of Bde Maka Ska and Lake Harriet. Cleveland's resulting plan connected the points of natural beauty of both sites. The Lake Calhoun Refectory was added in 1911, featuring restrooms and changing areas for visitors to the lake; it was renovated in the late 1990s.

Hennepin History Museum

2303 3rd Avenue S
Minneapolis, MN 55404
(612) 870-1329
www.hennepinhistory.org

The Hennepin History Museum is dedicated entirely to the history of Hennepin County and its residents through its exhibitions, library and educational programs. Hennepin History Museum is located in the George H. Christian House. The mansion's construction began in 1917. Then, George died. His son also died while overseeing construction. Nevertheless, when construction was completed, George Christian's widow moved in with her three adopted children.

A massive iron ornamental front door is the focal point of the exterior of the English Tudor–style mansion with ivy climbing the walls. On entering, visitors are met by the impressive Indiana limestone stairwell and the carved handrails.

On January 24, 1958, the Hennepin County History Museum opened. Rooms in the massive mansion were gradually filled with the forty thousand historical artifacts that moved into the building. The museum had occupied a "tired old building" (1516 Harmon Place) before moving. One item salvaged was "the Angel Gabriel," a weathervane made of sheet iron. It capped the Winslow House cupola and then the Minneapolis Industrial Exposition.

5

THE ARCHITECTURE OF
MINNEAPOLIS PUBLIC INSTITUTIONS

L ocal philanthropists, not surprisingly lumber and flour barons,
seeded Minneapolis public institutions. Local captains of
industry supported the arts and libraries, amassing paintings and
sculptures for closed upper-class society exhibitions. At first displayed in
homes, private collections grew and were shared at the public library and
then at art institutions. Art institutions, like Swan Turnblad's American
Swedish Institute (ASI), were organized with a singular vision. Another
institution with a single visionary was the Walker Art Center, conceived
by Thomas B. Walker. Still others, such as the Minneapolis Institute of
Art, were the collaborative effort of numerous wealthy philanthropists
from the start.

Lumberman Thomas B. Walker led the movement with public viewings
of art at the library. In 1877, art loan exhibitions began in Minneapolis.
Over thirty wealthy families presented 50 oil paintings as well as etchings
and engravings at Brigham House (Hennepin Avenue and 5th Street) on
September 25, 1878. In 1882, Ella S. Martin, the wife of a partner at
Washburn, Crosby and Company, led a fine art study group. In 1883, there
was another art loan exhibition in a commercial building, with an impressive
250 paintings and 125 etchings and engravings.

Before the Minneapolis Institute of Arts (Mia) forays into art, the
Athenaeum was the first cultural institution in Minneapolis. It was a "private
subscription" for "paying members."

Spoonbridge and Cherry, with the Basilica of St. Mary in the background, at the Walker Sculpture Garden.

Mayor Alonzo C. Rand's house hosted art lectures. Emma Crosby founded the Minneapolis Society of Fine Arts with fourteen men and eleven women. In 1883, University of Minnesota president William W. Folwell presided over the Minneapolis Society of Fine Arts. Walker pushed for public access of the Athenaeum by making the reading room free. In 1885, he led the public library that replaced the Athenaeum, also a free public institution. In a complex arrangement, the Minneapolis Public Library and the Athenaeum merged for ninety-nine years. The Minneapolis Library Board was established for oversight in 1885.

Until the construction of Mia, the library served as the society's exhibition space. Clinton Morrison donated his mansion Villa Rosa (3rd Avenue and 24th Avenue E) for Mia. In 1908, the ten-acre site was valued at $200,000. Walker vehemently objected, arguing the location was too far from downtown. On April 7, 1911, state legislation passed for the city to maintain the parkland. Mia accepted the gift and opened in 1915.

The Walker Art Center realized Thomas Walker's vision—an art center closer to downtown. Today, it is not that much closer, but Minneapolis won the argument—with two world-class art museums.

Thomas Barlow Walker's eponymous art collection opened to the public in 1874. In the 1880s, a small gallery opened free of charge to the public adjoining his home. In 1885, the Minneapolis Public Library Board opened with Walker as president. He was allowed to display his art in the library. Surprisingly, during this time, ads regularly ran in the local newspapers. For example, an ad ran in the *Minneapolis Journal* under "Amusements" and "Annual Art Exhibit" about the two hundred paintings by "leading American artists" at the public library from 10:00 a.m. to 10:00 p.m. with admission twenty-five cents for adults and ten cents for children.

During territorial days, the Athenaeum and the Minneapolis Library originated in Minneapolis. In 1849, William R. Marshall wrote the bill for the Minnesota territorial legislature incorporating the St. Anthony Library.

The St. Anthony Library Association was organized the following year. There were fifty shareholders with two hundred books and lyceum lectures. In 1853, a public reading room was established. William W. Wales owned a bookstore with a circulating library one could join for three dollars per annum in the Spooner Building on Main Street SE. At the bookstore, J. Hechtman succeeded Wales. In 1858, the Young Man's Library Association

Walker Art Center.

Minneapolis Institute of Art (Mia).

received three hundred books. The new public library was at Woodman's Hall on May 16, 1859. The Young Man's Library Association held lectures and literary events in 1859.

In 1860, "a private circulating library," the first Athenaeum, was founded with the financial help of shareholders—mostly upper-class elites. Thomas Hale Williams was both a bookseller and librarian. His bookstore in Bridge Square had amassed 250 volumes by 1861. In 1866, the Athenaeum opened at 215 Hennepin Avenue after $11,000 was raised.

Herbert Putnam served as first director of the Minneapolis Athenaeum (1884–87) and of the Minneapolis Public Library (1887–91). The son of George Putnam, the renowned New York publisher and a Harvard graduate, he later served four decades as librarian of Congress. From the 1870s through 1880s, there was a debate whether the library is a "scholarly preserve" or a "popular place." Eventually, the popular place won out, but not without the obvious need for intellectual sustenance of the written word for everyone, even the uneducated masses of working people.

Architects Franklin Long (1842–1912) and Frederick Kees drew the plans for the first Minneapolis Public Library (1889). The L-shaped (originally) and three-story Richardsonian Romanesque–style library (at 10th Street and Hennepin Avenue) resembled the Lumber Exchange Building, with brown Lake Superior sandstone on the exterior. The large foyer cost $324,893.57. In the fundraising campaign, Walker, Thomas Lowry, William S. King, William D. Washburn and Charles A. Pillsbury donated $5,000 each. The top floor featured an art gallery with paintings donated by James J. Hill, Thomas Lowry and, of course, Walker. The library was demolished in 1959.

Branch libraries were in established at North Minneapolis, in the basement of North High School and on Franklin Avenue in 1890. Carnegie libraries were constructed for the Franklin Branch (1914). The Central Branch was a Carnegie library that replaced New Boston in 1915 but has since been demolished and replaced.

In his memoir *Journey for Our Times*, Pulitzer Prize–winning journalist Harrison Salisbury described the Sumner Branch, the "immigrant's university." "Here in the United States, you could walk into the Sumner Branch Library and read what you wanted. No questions asked. If they didn't have the book you wanted, they would get it. That, I said, was one of the elements of American strength and the genius of the American idea." Minneapolis branch libraries served communities by making immigrants and their children citizens. In *North Side Memories*, Pacey Beers

Open Book Minneapolis.

reinforced Salisbury's statement: "Sumner Branch [Library]…was a wonderful place to go. It's still there, this Tudor Mansion…They had a large Yiddish collection. They were open on Sunday so that everybody—Jewish gentlemen who were observant on the Sabbath or who had work on the Sabbath—could…use the facility on Sunday afternoon."

In the Powderhorn neighborhood, the Hosmer Branch honored the library director James Hosmer in 1916. The Walker library branch, in the heart of Uptown, opened on land donated by Thomas B. Walker. In Minnehaha Park, the Longfellow Branch was the most unusual branch library in the Minneapolis Public Library system. The three-quarter-scale replica of Henry Wadsworth Longfellow House was gifted by Robert "Fish" Jones. Once an attraction at Jones's zoo, it served as a branch library from 1937 to 1968.

Hosmer (1834–1937) was library director from 1892 to 1904. The Harvard grad and professor was a writer and historian who left the day-to-day activities of operating the library to his assistant Gratia A. Countryman.

Countryman was born in Hastings, Minnesota, and educated as a teacher; for a time, she was a substitute. She studied music and literature part time with Professor Maria Sanford—a trailblazer for women in academia as the first female college instructor at the University of Minnesota. Countryman, on the recommendation of both Putnam and Hosmer, was elevated to head librarian in 1904. However, she earned $1,000 for the position, while previous holders received $3,000 annually, as the only American woman overseeing a large library collection and system.

Libraries allowed a few women to break the glass ceiling. For example, in 1896, Jennie C. Crays was the first female member of the library board. She was also a veteran of the Minneapolis School Board. Moreover, in 1934, Gratia A. Countryman was elected, at the height of the Depression, chairman of the American Library Association. Countryman's mission was democratizing the library. All citizens, regardless of socioeconomic status, were included. In 1905, the library aimed a program at factories, where workers borrowed books.

In 1961, the Minneapolis Public Library on 10th Street was replaced. It was relocated to the present site, where two structures have stood. The first library existed from 1961 to 2002. In 2008, under financial distress, the Athenaeum (today, housed on the fourth floor) and Minneapolis Public Library joined the Hennepin County Library system.

Weisman Art Museum.

The latest Minneapolis Public Library (2006) was conceived by world-renowned Argentine American architect Cesar Pelli. It was renamed the Hennepin County Library after the merger (2008). Sunlight shone through the building's abundant glass but especially in the huge atrium between five stories piled on one side and four stories on the other.

In St. Anthony, college education was a major concern. In territorial days, the legislature determined St. Anthony as the site of the "state university." St. Paul received the capitol and Stillwater the penitentiary.

Territorial legislator John W. North wrote the bill. When signed into law, "the state university" received an endowment on February 13, 1851. Franklin Steele donated four acres for the University of Minnesota. A two-story frame building was a preparatory academy for the university. For three years, Reverend E.W. Merrill led the school. It failed due to impossible financial circumstances.

The *St. Anthony Express* regularly ran an ad for the preparatory school. The October 15, 1852 issue stated, "The Fall term will commence on Wednesday, October 13." The eleven-week quarter tuition was staggered based on academic discipline: "Primary Dependent," three dollars; "common English branches," four dollars; "language and higher mathematics," six dollars; these were some of the academic offerings. The ad was signed by E.W. Merrill, principal.

By 1856, Steele's "financial and legal affairs" as stated in *St. Anthony Falls Rediscovered*, necessitated the University of Minnesota's relocation. However, the Panic of 1857 caused by the Ohio Life Insurance and Trust Company led to a money shortage and financial stagnation. It was followed by the Civil War; the university's plans were put on hold. In 1856, the University of Minnesota moved to its present-day site, and Old Main, the first building, was constructed. In 1862, the U.S. government passed the (Justin) Morrill Act, which funded land grant and agricultural colleges. For each congressional district, thirty thousand acres were allotted.

William Watts Folwell served as first University of Minnesota president (1869–84). From upstate New York, after a stint as a math professor at Hobart College, he was lured to the state university in 1869, the first year the school accepted college students. Later, he would become the first state historian.

The University of Minnesota was co-educational from the start. A student, Harrison Salisbury, described the university: "The University of Minnesota in the 1920s was a meat and potatoes institution; it gave you the facts and figures. If you wanted to become a dentist, a doctor, a pharmacist, a chemist, an engineer or a farmer, this was the place."

Guthrie Theater.

In 1961, ground was broken for Blegen Hall and two administrative buildings (Social Science and Business). Since then, the West Bank of the University of Minnesota has grown to encompass a significant portion of Cedar-Riverside.

The Baldwin School, later Macalester College, has roots in St. Anthony at the Winslow House. The Baldwin School was a preparatory school for Macalester College. In June 1853, the first Baldwin School opened in St. Paul.

The Winslow House opened in 1857. The hotel had served as a summer retreat in the Northwest for southern plantation owners before the Civil War. In 1872, the forerunner to Macalester College rented Winslow House. It was owned by Charles Macalester, an old Philadelphia acquaintance of Edward D. Neill who had returned from Europe. In 1881, the college relocated to then farmland on Grand Avenue in St. Paul, in the present-day Macalester-Groveland neighborhood.

In 1871, the predecessor of Augsburg University relocated from Marshall, Wisconsin. Originally operating as a seminary, the institution was formerly the Norwegian Danish Evangelical Lutheran Augsburg Seminary. Today, Augsburg University is a private liberal arts school of higher education known for Norwegian heritage and community service.

YOUR GUIDE TO HISTORY

American Swedish Institute

2600 Park Avenue S
Minneapolis, MN 55407
(612) 871-4907
www.asimn.org
$12 adults; $8 seniors ages 62 and above; $6 ages 6–18 and full-time
   students with ID

The American Swedish Institute is the former residence of the Turnblad family. Swan, Christina and their daughter, Lillian, lived in the house from 1908 to 1929. Swan Turnblad was the publisher of the largest Swedish language newspaper in the United States, *Svenska Amerikanska Posten*.

Guthrie Theatre

818 2nd Street S
Minneapolis, MN 55415
(612) 225-6000
www.guthrietheater.org

The Guthrie Theater was founded by Sir Tyrone Guthrie in 1963. Formerly part of the Walker Art Center, in the 1970s, it moved into its current location in 2006. The theater offers musical, theatrical and dance performances year-round, with an emphasis on supporting local talent and promoting social issues through art.

John Cowles of the Star-Tribune newspaper was instrumental in convincing Sir Tyrone Guthrie to locate his eponymous theater in Minneapolis. The first beloved theater stood beside the Walker Art Center, but it was razed for expansion of gallery space. The new Guthrie was pivotal in rehabilitating the Minneapolis riverfront.

Minneapolis College of Art and Design (MCAD)

2501 Stevens Avenue
Minneapolis, MN 55404
(612) 874-3760
mcad.edu

Founded by the Society of Fine Arts as the Minneapolis Institute of Arts in 1915, MCAD was one of the first schools in the country to offer an accreditation in the arts. Originally founded as the Minneapolis School of Fine Arts in April 15, 1886, the institute was located in a house on

Hennepin. The first art school students enrolled in 1886 under the tutelage of Douglas Volk (at Hennepin Avenue and 10th Street). In 1889, the school moved into the Minneapolis Public Library. The school of art relocated to the iconic Julia Morrison Memorial Building in 1916. In 1970, the Minneapolis School of Fine Arts was renamed the Minneapolis College of Art and Design.

Minnesota Institute of Arts (Mia)
2400 3rd Avenue S
Minneapolis, MN 55404
(888) 642-2787
artsmia.org

The prestigious New York architecture firm McKim, Mead & White created Mia's first design. In 1916, Edwin Hewitt and Edwin Brown built an addition. Kenzo Tange, with the Parker Klein Association, followed in 1974 and the Minneapolis College of Art and Design (MCAD) and the Children's Theater Company in 1972. The complex united Minneapolis Institute of Fine Arts with MCAD. Finally, Michael Graves added another addition in 2006.

Minneapolis St. Paul International Film Festival
The Film Society of Minneapolis St. Paul
125 SE Main Street, Suite 341
Minneapolis, MN 55414
(612) 331-7563
MSPIFF mspfilm.org/festivals/mspiff
See site for ticket prices

Every April, Film Society of Minneapolis St. Paul organizes and hosts the Minneapolis St. Paul International Film Festival. As the largest international cinema event in the region, more than 250-plus films from some seventy countries are shown during the festival, drawing audiences of fifty thousand plus.

The Museum of Russian Art
5500 Stevens Avenue S
Minneapolis, MN 55419
(612) 821-9045
$10 adults; children under 14 and students $5
tmora.org

The Museum of Russian Art houses the largest permanent collection of Russian art in North America. Some of its exhibitions have included artifacts from prehistoric Russia, poster art of the Russian Revolution and illuminated manuscripts from the early Eastern Orthodox Church.

The Open Book

1011 Washington Avenue S
Minneapolis, MN 55415
(612) 215-2650
openbookmn.org

The riverfront renaissance occurred in the arts as well. The Open Book opened in a rehabbed building for the Loft Literary Center, which has occupied numerous sites since its inception in 1974; Milkweed Editions; and the Minnesota Center for Book Arts on Washington Avenue just outside of downtown.

In 2008, Sharon Sayles Belton said about the Open Book in the MRROHP, "We had, a few years back, as you might recall, made an investment in Open Book at the far end. When I went to groundbreaking of Open Book, I said to them, 'You guys are at the east end of the renaissance that will occur on Washington Avenue. It will take time, and if you look out the door right now, it doesn't look like it, but just mark my words.' I was at Open Book last year for a poetry reading and the gentleman who is running Open Book repeated that story to the people who were in the audience. 'We were the first on the block.'"

Walker Art Center

725 Vineland Place
Minneapolis, MN 55403
(612) 375-7600
walkerart.org
$25 adults; children under 18 free

In 1924, the Walker Art Gallery commenced construction. The first building was completed in an unusual Byzantine and Spanish style in 1928. By 1940, the gallery had been renovated to convey its position as a purveyor of modern art, architecture and the avant-garde. In 1969, the old art museum was leveled to make room for a larger building.

The Walker hired Edward Larrabee Barnes, a modern architect, to design the galleries. His layout was designed for museum visitors and reflected his study with Bauhaus masters Walter Gropius and Marcel

Breuer. The Walker design made use of minimalist blank rectangles with brown-purple bricks.

In 2005, the Walker Art Center added ten thousand square feet of exhibition space. Swiss architects Jacques Herzog and Pierre de Meuron designed the addition and renovation.

Weisman Art Museum

333 East River Road
Minneapolis, MN 55455
(612) 625-9494
wam.umn.edu

The Weisman Art Museum, designed by Frank Gehry, opened in 1993. Located on the campus of the University of Minnesota, the museum's stated mission is to support art that sparks discovery, critical thinking and transformation.

The Frederick R. Weisman Art Museum presents the University of Minnesota art. It is collected in one museum with architectural design provided by Frank Gehry, who is one of the world's most well-known architects.

6

CEMETERIES AND PARKS

Until the nineteenth century, wealthy parishioners were buried beside their respective churches in the grounds. Churchyards were overcrowded as urbanism increased, and public health concerns were raised. In St. Anthony, the first recorded cemetery was in the middle of a residential neighborhood, on 5th Avenue and 8th Street SE.

In 1849, in St. Anthony Township, Robert W. Cummings acquired property for the city's first cemetery. In 1853, Maple Hill Cemetery included over twenty acres, but ten acres were added to the adjoining Cummings addition. In February 1857, Maple Hill Cemetery was dedicated, and approximately five thousand bodies were buried there before 1890.

The surrounding neighborhood's density increased, which resulted in various problems before the cemetery closed. The *Minneapolis Tribune* wrote on March 3, 1889, that the cemetery "in the residence portion of the city" was "a serious menace to health." The paper continued, "Dr. Klivington, in his report to the city council on the Maple Hill Cemetery as to its menace to health, did not exaggerate the matter, for all that he said is supported by the testimony of some of the oldest and most influential citizens of the East side who have interested themselves in having the cemetery removed from its present location....Dr. Klivington says that a great many bodies are buried there at the present time because it is cheap."

In 1890, city health officials ended burials and converted the former cemetery into parkland. As the cemetery stood on higher ground, it was feared the interments could pollute local wells. After the cemetery

Heffelfinger Fountain at the Lyndale Park Rose Garden.

closed, 1,300 bodies were disinterred. Later, the park was named after Italian jurist and author Giacomo Beltrami, who explored the source of the Mississippi River.

The *Minneapolis Tribune* wrote of "Rejuvenation of Old Maple Hill Cemetery Now Being Accomplished" on September 27, 1908: "A transformation scene is going on in Maple Hill Cemetery at Broadway and Polk streets northeast, where workmen employed by the park board are engaged in effecting improvements for which the city council a few months ago, appropriated $5,000." Then the article described the neglect: "The cemetery was never kept up as cemeteries are expected to be, and this together with its being near the heart of the city has caused it to be the occasion of much disputation, legislation and litigation for many years."

Pioneers and Soldiers Cemetery began as Layman's Cemetery. Isaac Layman, the son of Martin, said his father purchased the farmland for $1,000 in 1852. In 1883, the first burial at the twenty-seven-acre cemetery occurred.

The Lyndale Cemetery Association was founded by George Brackett, Charles M. Loring, Dorilus Morrison, William D. Washburn, William King and others in 1871. The cemetery was, once part of King's 1,400-acre Lyndale Farms, a country estate from present-day 34th Street to Lake Harriet between Lyndale and Hennepin Avenues. Other portions of the farm were later donated for Lake Harriet Park and King's Highway. The land was purchased for $21,000 with an additional $4,000 for improvements. In 1872, the trustees renamed the property Lakewood Cemetery. Lakewood Cemetery was originally 128 acres. In 1874, an additional 24½ acres were purchased, with 50 more added in 1893, to the present size of 250 acres. As it was then outside of the city limit, the founders contended the cemetery would remain forever. Lakewood was publicly dedicated as nondenominational on September 16, 1872.

Modeled after Père Lachaise—the nineteenth-century French cemetery located on 48 acres outside of Paris—Lakewood Cemetery expanded to 110 acres. Its winding serpentine roads, meadows and forest were used as picnic grounds, like many other cemeteries throughout the country, when parkland was rare.

Lakewood Cemetery also was inspired by Grove Street Cemetery in New Haven, Connecticut. Originally the New Haven Burying Ground, it opened in 1796 on only six acres. But Spring Grove in Cincinnati, Ohio, provided the template for Lakewood Cemetery, with simple yet stylized natural landscape design.

Pioneer and Soldiers Cemetery.

The *Minneapolis Journal* contained the headline "No Grave-Robbing Here" on October 10, 1907. The cemetery superintendent A.W. Hobert reported "it could not escape detection." The article continued: Hobert said he was "not greatly disturbed on the sensational report in a morning paper that the ghoulish traffic of body-snatching is going on without restraint in Minneapolis." He concluded, "It would be impossible for grave robbers to ply their trade in Lakewood Cemetery and escape detection."

The Minneapolis Park System, like the local cemeteries, heavily borrowed organizational ideas from the East Coast. Charles M. Loring, the "Father of the Park System" of Minneapolis, exemplified this tradition.

In 1833, Loring was born in Maine, but he moved to Minneapolis in 1860. On arrival, his future business partner, Loren Fletcher, had rented the adjoining room in the Nicollet Hotel. In *Old Rail Fence Corners*, Loring fondly recalled future parkland: "There was a cranberry marsh a half mile west of Lake Calhoun [Bde Maka Ska], on what is now Lake Street, where we used to gather berries." He sold supplies to lumberman with Fletcher. Later, he was a member of the U.S. House of Representatives, as well as an owner of the Galaxy and Minnetonka Mill. Loring also was a secretary of the Athenaeum. In the 1870s, he served on the city council and helped found Lakewood Cemetery in 1871. As Loring's health declined, and he wintered in Europe and, later, Riverside, California.

In 1883, the Minneapolis Park Board was established. The Minneapolis Park Board, as David C. Smith said in *City of Parks: The Story of Minneapolis*, is an "independent public entity," supported by city taxes.

Before the merger of Minneapolis and St. Anthony, efforts were already underway to reserve parkland. In 1857, Murphy's Square was the first attempt at a city park. Then located outside the city limit, it is now on the Augsburg University campus on the claim of Edward Murphy. It extended to the river flats, and Murphy once bragged of owning over five hundred lots and three hundred acres of property. His land was "The only public square in Town" and "donated by me," he said in an 1859 advertisement in the *Minnesota State News*. He believed the park would spark demand for lots surrounding the square, but sales remained slow.

In 1883, Central Park opened in Minneapolis. Surrounded by "garden farms"—farms that grew vegetables for sale—the Minneapolis park was renamed in Loring's honor in 1891. In 1856, Joseph S. Johnson claimed 160 acres including present-day Loring Park and Loring Lake, originally Johnson's Lake.

Nicollet Island was another unsuccessful attempt at acquiring city parkland. "Remember Nicollet Island" was a refrain repeated by city leaders for decades. In 1866, voters disapproved a merger of Minneapolis and St. Anthony, with Nicollet Island at the center, with city buildings and a public park on the 118-acre site. But, at the ballot box, voters refused to pay the price, and both the merger and the park were defeated.

Horace W.S. Cleveland's (1814–1900) first landscape architecture designs involved cemeteries, for example, Sleepy Hollow on New York's Hudson River. Earlier in his career, Cleveland worked for Ralph Waldo Emerson and Frederick Law Olmsted. But in Minneapolis, his vision was behind the nationally recognized park system. Minneapolis's first cemetery association organized on September 14, 1854.

Cleveland arrived from Chicago at the then advanced age of fifty-eight years old. He developed the blueprint for parks in Minneapolis. Loring expanded on Cleveland's plans by acquiring parkland with the support of the park board on Lake of the Isles, Minnehaha; Saratoga Park in 1889; then Glenwood Park, with the first 53 acres of the future Theodore Wirth Park; as well as Victory Memorial and St. Anthony Parkways. Also added were parks in city council wards, for example, First Ward Park, later renamed Logan Park. In addition, there was Sixth Ward Park, 25 acres that later became known as Riverside Park. As Smith said regarding the leadership of Loring, "In the space of just over ten years the park board had acquired 1,476 acres

Downtown Minneapolis from Loring Park.

of land and water." Despite his professional success with the park board, Loring's personal fortune declined, and he declared bankruptcy in 1895.

In 1896, Theodore Wirth (1863–1949) was hired from Hartford, Connecticut, "the oldest municipal park system." A native of Switzerland, Wirth replaced William Berry, who was the first to hold the title of superintendent of Minneapolis Parks. Unlike minimalist landscape architects such Olmsted and Cleveland, Wirth was a maximalist and freely modified the natural landscape: building parkways, planting gardens and repeatedly dredging. Minneapolis parkland doubled between 1907 and 1910.

Wirth improved the Minneapolis Chain of Lakes: Lake of the Isle, Bde Maka Ska, Lake Harriet, Lake Nokomis (then Amelia) and Lake Hiawatha, then a marsh. Dredging was extensively used in creating more stable lakes and efficacious environs for attracting developers and residential housing. Before improvements, the swampy Lake of the Isles was a poor land for a residential neighborhood. But after the park board's investment in dredging and landscaping, the neighborhood was one of the most affluent in the city. In 1906, Wirth improved Lake of Isles from 100 acres of shallow water, 67 acres of swamps and 33 acres of dry land to 120 acres of water and 80 acres of dry land in 1911. In addition, Lake Nokomis was reduced from 300 to 200 acres between 1914 and 1918.

Minnehaha Park's creation was an ongoing process with fits and starts over several decades. In 1868, St. Paul, St. Anthony and Minneapolis passed a resolution to purchase Fort Snelling and Minnehaha Falls. But the joint effort withdrew after they failed to raise the necessary funds. In 1889, Minnehaha could have become the first state park and second in the nation, but the Minnesota legislature lacked appropriations to purchase the parkland. However, the Minneapolis Park Board approached the city elites; the group raised enough money for the legislature to transfer the title. Over time, it was paid off by the city taxpayers, and Minnehaha Park was born.

After the 1880s, the park board's focus changed. Sports and recreation gained traction. The aesthetics of parkland began to include athletic fields. In addition, music was performed at parks, plus there was ice skating, biking, boating and more. Then, at the beginning of the twentieth century, the playground movement recalibrated parks. Attention was focused on children's well-being; sandboxes and maypoles were added. But the first playgrounds were dangerous and not designed for small children.

In 1887, after persuading the state legislature, the park board was allowed to provide its own police force and to control all tree care on city streets. This

Boating on Lake of the Isles.

assertion of independence protected the park board and park system from the possibly corrupt influence of the police force and city hall.

In the early 1900s, the Minneapolis Park Board lagged behind major cities in recreation amenities. The park board reacted by improving opportunities. First, some parks were equipped with gymnastics equipment. The Parade (adjoining and also part of the present-day the Walker Sculpture Garden) was designated for physical education and team sports. Within the city, team sports began organizing in 1908. In 1915, Glenwood Golf nine-hole course opened. It was followed by Armour (later Gross) and Rice Lake (later Hiawatha) golf courses. In 1924, ski jumping trials for the Winter Olympics were held at Glenwood Park. Speed skating was hosted at Powderhorn Park in 1936. Eventually, reflecting the modern demands of the system, the organization was renamed Minneapolis Parks and Recreation Board (MPRB).

The MPRB grew to encompass twelve lakes, the Mississippi River, three tributary streams and sixty miles of Grand Rounds parkways. The MPRB owns the city land on the water, except for the land north of Broadway Avenue. William W. Folwell envisioned and coined the name "Grand Rounds," an amenity accessible that displayed the vision and beauty of the entire City of Lakes. But on the neighborhood level, the MPRB accomplished another major goal—a park was within a half mile of every residence by the 1970s.

YOUR GUIDE TO HISTORY

Eloise Butler Wildflower Garden and Bird Sanctuary
1 Theodore Wirth Parkway
Minneapolis, MN 55422
(612) 230-6400
www.minneapolisparks.org
Free

In early 1907, Eloise Butler petitioned the park board for space to establish a botanical garden. The park board granted the request and set aside three acres of bog, meadow and hillside for the Wild Botanical Garden—now the Eloise Butler Wildflower Garden and Bird Sanctuary— the first public wildflower garden in the United States. The park is a true natural habitat in the middle of an urban landscape. It offers a floating walkway that takes you past the nesting grounds of wood ducks, red-wing blackbirds and a variety of other native birds and animals that make the park their home.

Fort Snelling National Cemetery
7601 34th Avenue S
Minneapolis, MN 55450
(612) 726 1127
www.cem.va.gov/CEMs/nchp/ftsnelling.asp

Fort Snelling National Cemetery is the final resting place for members of the armed forces and their eligible spouses and children.

Lakewood Cemetery
3600 Hennepin Avenue S
Minneapolis, MN 55408
(612) 822-2171
www.lakewoodcemetery.org

Founded in 1871, Lakewood Cemetery is the final home for many of Minneapolis's most prominent citizens, politicians and families. Some of the notable people buried here are Vice President Hubert Humphrey, Dunwoody Institute founder William Dunwoody, musician Tiny Tim and suffragette Clara Ueland. Memorials to the Grand Army of the Republic, the Brotherhood of the Fraternal Order of Elks and the Washburn A Mill Explosion Memorial Obelisk can also be found on the grounds.

Pioneers & Soldiers Memorial Cemetery

2945 Cedar Avenue S
Minneapolis, MN 55407
(612) 729-8484
www.friendsofthecemetery.org
Free, open April 15 to October 15

Since the first burial in 1853, Pioneers & Soldiers Memorial Cemetery (formerly Layman's Cemetery) is the final resting place for over twenty thousand of Minneapolis's first residents, including early settlers, African Americans and members of the abolitionist movement, veterans of the War of 1812 to World War I and several thousand immigrants from Scandinavia and Eastern Europe; more than ten thousand of the graves belong to children. The graves of many prominent territorial pioneers, including Charles Christmas, Edwin Hedderly and Philander Prescott, can be found here. Because only about one out of every nine graves is marked, a visit to the caretaker's office to see the cemetery's plat book is necessary if you're looking for a specific grave. In 2002, the cemetery was given the designation of a Historic Place by the National Register of Historic Places.

7

SETTLERS AND IMMIGRATION AND RELIGIOUS INSTITUTIONS

Minnesota and St. Anthony offered ample opportunities for settlers and immigrants alike. The Homestead Act (1862) provided U.S. citizens 160 acres when a residence was maintained. The settlers staked claims and were required to "improve the land" for five years and pay a ten-dollar filing fee. Booster literature was used to lure immigrants. In 1853, Bond wrote, "The territory *must* be peopled, and even the very rapid immigration from outside does not do it fast enough."

Old Stock Americans were the largest groups to first migrate to Minneapolis. They were primarily New Englanders, New Yorkers and from the middle states. In the nineteenth century, the Old Stock Americans were the elites and were elected to most political positions. Later, with conservative Scandinavians, they formed a coalition to retain power against labor backing Irish and Germans in the last decades of the century. About the Irish, Green said in *A Peculiar Imbalance*, "During the early 1850s Minnesotans created a society in which Irish Catholics, the least acculturated and most derided of whites by the Yankee elite, were granted political rights but afforded limited opportunities to economic development and relegated to fill the city's laboring class." The Scandinavians challenged the Yankees while representing all political stripes in the twentieth century. In St. Anthony, the Old Stock abolitionists and prohibitionists reached their apex in cultural and political dominance. Many of the Old Stock settlers dreamed of a New England town and biblical "a City upon a Hill."

Our Lady of Lourdes.

There were small numbers of freedmen living in Minnesota Territory. In 1857, St. Anthony had eight black families; many resided in the basement of the Winslow House. From 1860 to 1875, the third and fourth wards of St. Anthony were areas of black settlement. Between 1870 and 1930, African Americans also relocated to Nicollet Avenue and 10th Street S. In 1910, African Americans moved from Seven Corners to the North Side. African American settlement patterns followed that of another other group that faced persistent discrimination—the Jews. Both faced an extreme paucity of available housing accommodations limited to undesirable sections of the city. Despite real estate agents' discriminatory efforts, African American found housing in neighborhoods of all thirteen city wards.

African Americans encountered discrimination in all aspects of life in Minneapolis. However, organized labor allowed a few opportunities for African Americans. But for the most part, they struggled collectively for improved wages and work conditions. In 1925, African American union organizer Nellie Stone Johnson (1905–2002) found employment at the Minneapolis Athletic Club as an elevator operator. During her years as a union organizer, she had connections with communists. So Hubert Humphrey, a fervid anti-communist, asked her advice on the topic. She was instrumental in the Democratic Party and Farmer-Labor Party merger in Democratic-Farmer-Labor Party in cooperation with Humphrey. In 1945, she was elected to the Minneapolis Library Board. In her lifetime, Nellie Stone Johnson was one of numerous African Americans who improved her community and Minneapolis at large.

In 1851, the first Swedish immigrant in Minneapolis was a shoemaker from Skåne. He settled north of St. Anthony on the river flats. After 1870, the Swedish population dramatically increased in "Swede towns."

Minneapolis attracted Scandinavians who promoted the area for settlement. Famous Swedish novelist and feminist Fredrika Bremer visited in 1850. Norway's great violinist Ole Bull also toured. Hans Mattson was an agent for the railroads. Mattson encouraged immigration to the region through pamphlets and the powerful influence of the Swedish press.

From 1880 to 1910, Cedar-Riverside was the largest Swedish community in Minneapolis. In that time, the community's roots extended just east of the Milwaukee Road Depot. Snoose Boulevards, or *snusgatan*, developed in the neighborhood. As David A. Lanegran described in *Swedes in the Twin Cities*, "There were two Snoose Boulevards here: Washington Avenue, which had become the district where lumberjacks, farmhands, and other seasonal workers as well as the homeless or unemployed, hung out; and Cedar Avenue, which was lined with Scandinavian businesses, saloons, and theaters." From the start, despite the sober reputation of Swedes, there reputation was broken, "Att gå på"—translated from Swedish as "go down to Cedar" (to drink!) was the cry on the street. And along with drinking, allied businesses—prostitution and bootlegging—also flourished. In Cedar-Riverside, several businesses and theaters had enduring legacies; some of them included C.J. Samuelsons, Holtzermanns, Dania Hall and the Southern Theater.

Northeast Minneapolis was another destination for Swedes. Flour mills, breweries, railroad repair shops and foundries attracted workers. The Swedes once dominated the neighborhoods in Maple Hill, Columbia Park and Pierce Street in an area known as "Swede Alley." The group had a staying power, too; until the 1930s, Swedes were the largest immigrant group in ward nine in Northeast Minneapolis.

After 1900, another group of Swedes settled in North Minneapolis. Around Shingle Creek in the Camden neighborhood, lumber milling and allied jobs provided a significant draw to Swedish immigrants and established residents. The C.A. Smith sawmill was Swedish owned.

However, over time, South Minneapolis had the greatest concentration of Swedes. Many moved south along the corridor of Cedar Avenue in the 1890s. Swedes also settled in the Seward and Powderhorn neighborhoods in huge numbers.

View of Downtown from North Minneapolis.

In 1895, the Sons of Norway was established in North Minneapolis by eighteen founders. The organization's advent signaled the community's rising standing in the city. It provided insurance to members as well as Norwegian culture.

Jews immigrated in much smaller numbers to Minneapolis. However, they had a lasting impact on Minneapolis business and politics. Their presence also highlighted a civic problem: systemic antisemitism and discrimination in Minneapolis.

In 1867's city directory, the first Jews listed in Minneapolis were E. Altman and S. Lauchheim, who sold wholesale and retail clothing in Bridge Square. The first Jewish settlement was a veld (farm) at 33rd and Dupont Avenue N in North Minneapolis. Many Jews from western Russia, or the Pale of Settlement, immigrated to Minneapolis. In the late nineteenth and early twentieth centuries, Jewish immigration was concentrated in three areas of Minneapolis: the North Side, North Minneapolis and along Franklin Avenue S and 15th Street S. Romanian Jews also established a small community in North Minneapolis.

In 1907, Jewish families congregated along Glenwood Avenue. By 1920, Willard Hay and Homewood had many Jewish immigrants. During that time, businesses were almost 100 percent Jewish on Plymouth Avenue. In *North Side Memories*, Linda Mack Schloff said, "Although both neighborhoods of the North Side were heavily Jewish, the area also was home to other ethnic groups. Finns lived along Glenwood Avenue to the south of 6th Avenue N; and along Broadway to the north of Plymouth Avenue, there were Irish and Poles. African-Americans in need of inexpensive housing moved into formerly Jewish housing on the near North Side during the 1920s." The Johnson-Reed Act (1924) closed immigration through a race-based quota system. There were forty thousand Jews in Minnesota, but most were eastern European.

Later, on the North Side, there was a small group of Russian, Polish and Lithuanians with similar culture affinity and faith near Washington Avenue and 5th Street N. Nearby, the street known as 6th Avenue N became Olson Memorial Highway in honor of Floyd B. Olson, the *shabbos goy*, who lighted stoves and turned on lights during the Sabbath and Jewish holidays.

Synagogues and Jewish institutions were established to meet the growing populations' needs. In 1875, the Montefiore Burial Society was founded by German Jews, later renamed Temple Israel Memorial Park. Another institution was the Bas Zion (Daughters of Zion)—a women's benevolent society.

Former Plymouth Avenue Bridge connecting Nicollet Island to old Saint Anthony.

In 1878, twenty-three members formed the Shaaroi Tov ("The Gates of Goodness") in a rented space. It became Temple Israel, first at 10th Street and 5th Avenue in 1888. In 1902, after a fire, it was rebuilt. That building lasted until 1928. Then the current site was constructed (2324 Emerson Avenue S). In 1880, the Minneapolis Jewish population was four thousand; it doubled to approximately eight thousand in 1900.

In 1875, Slovaks started working in the mills in Minneapolis, drawn to the area mistakenly believing Dr. Jacob Elliot's surname was Elias, a fellow countryman, and settled the neighborhood looking for jobs. Later known as Elliot Park, the parkland was donated by the doctor when he retired to California.

Bohemian Flats, first known as the Danish Flats, was below the Mississippi River bluffs. In the 1880s, Slovaks arrived on the flats, the west bank of the present-day University of Minnesota. Also included were Connemara Irish, Swedes, Danes and Germans. The Slovaks also built St. Cyril's Church in Northeast Minneapolis. The 1900 census revealed the diversity of the flats cut off from the city by geography: 613 Slovaks, 123 Swedes, 190 Czechs, 41 Irish, 27 Norwegians, 10 Poles, 5 Germans, 4 Austrians, 2 Danes, plus "mixed marriages." The poor but tight-knit

Boat launch at the Bohemian Flats.

community on the flood plain received the first of many condemnations in 1915; in 1931, the last residents were relocated for coal docks and a barge terminal.

Minnesota, and Minneapolis, had a small but tight-knit Italian population. It centered on the Maple Hill neighborhood, later renamed Beltrami Park. In Northeast Minneapolis, Beltrami was in area bordered by Fillmore Street in the west, Johnson Street in the east and Broadway Avenue in the north. The immigrants were from mostly the Calabria, Abruzzi and Mezzogiorno regions of Italy. As Rudolph J. Vecoli said in *They Chose Minnesota*, "The neighborhood was noted for its flourishing gardens and its variety of barnyard animals—important sources of food. With the exception of those few who established grocery stores or saloons, the Italians for the most part worked in the section gangs or the shops of the Soo Line Railroad."

The Greeks were another small, but influential, immigrant group. In 1910, there were only 463 in Minneapolis. But they lived in all thirteen wards by 1920. The local Greeks, following national trends, worked in diners and specialized in perfecting toothsome American fare such as burgers, fries and other homey foods at reasonable prices. Additionally, they also specialized in confections. The community found its spiritual life at St. Mary's Greek Orthodox Church. In 1909, the church moved to East Lake Street.

The Lebanese, then mostly Christians, settled first in Northeast Minneapolis. They were the first Middle Eastern immigrants in an area with an already diverse population. In 1978, 90 percent of immigrants from the Arab world were Christian Lebanese. The Lebanese were called Syrians until Lebanese statehood in 1926. In 1970, there were 243 Lebanese in Minneapolis—with 48 foreign born.

Chinese and Japanese were the first Asians in Minneapolis. Following the Chinese Exclusion Act (1882), the immigrant group dispersed from the west to perform the only jobs permitted by a discriminatory city. In 1885, Minneapolis had fourteen Chinese laundries, found largely in the Gateway District. Gradually, restaurants served heavily Americanized Chinese cuisine, and this was another employment option. The first Chinese restaurant in Minneapolis was the Canton Café on 1st Avenue S in 1883. The restaurant moved south to 6th Street, where it changed names to Yuen Faung Low ("exotic fragrance from afar") or John's Place, with imported Chinese décor. It was a local destination for years. In 1910, there were ten Chinese restaurants in Minneapolis.

The Japanese, like the Chinese, had escaped racism and discrimination. The 1924 Immigration Act included the Asian Exclusion Act. The law was the first step toward Executive Order 9066, signed by President Franklin Delano Roosevelt in 1942; through the order, Japanese Americans were deported to internment camps within the United States. As Michael Albert wrote in *They Chose Minnesota*, "The Japanese-American population of the Twin Cities in 1980 was largely a legacy of the language school. Relatives, wives, sweethearts, and friends of many of its students left the detention camps to reside in the Twin Cities during the six- or nine-month course. In a 1968 survey of metropolitan Nisei revealed that fully 50% had been stationed at Camp Savage or Fort Snelling or had a family member there." In 1946, Hubert Humphrey, as mayor of Minneapolis, said of the Japanese who attended the school, "It is a pleasure to note that many of them have chosen to make Minneapolis their permanent home,"

The Hmong fought alongside the United States and CIA against the Pathet Lao and Vietnamese Communists. As a result of the "Secret War" and the United States' defeat in Vietnam, the ethnic minority began to settle in Minnesota in 1976. The Hmong migrated from South China to Laos, Thailand and Vietnam in the early 1800s. But the Hmong who immigrated to the United States were from Laos. Slash-and-burn farmers without formal education, the Hmong practiced animism—a form of ancestor worship with highly developed rituals—until the 1950s. Gradually, some Hmong converted to various Christian faiths.

Over the years, 130,000 Hmong were resettled in the United States. In addition, there were 10,000 Hmong who immigrated to France, and 1,000 took refuge in Canada and Australia. In the 1970s, Hmong were resettled with an American "sponsor." The sponsor provided necessities when refugees arrived. In the 1980s, "chain migration" began and was finally realized with "family reunification" in many cases. Minnesota has a strong faith-based resettlement program with two major organizations: the Lutheran Immigrant and Refugee Service (LIRS) and the U.S. Catholic Conference (USCC). Catholic Charities works with the USCC in resettlement of refugees. The Hmong resettlement patterns in the Twin Cities, as Chia Youyee Vang said in *The Hmong in Minnesota*, "Like other immigrant groups, Hmong refugees were concentrated in poor, urban neighborhoods, including Phillips and Near North in Minneapolis and Frogtown in St. Paul." In Minneapolis, the Sumner Field Housing Project was the first home to many Hmong.

St. Paul is recognized nationally as a Hmong city. But Minneapolis is also an important regional destination. As Sarah R. Mason said, "The majority in the Twin Cities settled initially in the Summit-University area of St. Paul and, by 1979, in south Minneapolis."

Minneapolis's most recent wave of immigrants was not the first to search for succor. One in fourteen city residents, whether occasionally or daily, relied on settlements for essential community services, as the *Minneapolis Tribune* explained on May 29, 1921: "a vast amount of valuable help is given the members of the community through free clinics and employment bureaus, kindergartens, day nurseries and friendly visiting." The paper listed Northeast, Pillsbury, Wells, Unity, Margaret Berry, Talmud Torah and Washington neighborhood houses. Most settlement houses were of a transitory nature and came and went and consolidated as neighborhoods and communities' needs evolved.

Through religious institutions, migrants and immigrants found a new home in Minneapolis. The religious institutions tied both migrants and immigrants to their past. The institutions also created communities for the future. The following is a brief survey of the historic churches and synagogues in Minneapolis, with a focus on historic architecture.

In St. Anthony, St. Anthony of Padua was the first Catholic church. Father Augustine Ravoux, the itinerant priest was sent to preach to the Dakota in Minnesota Territory. In 1848, Ravoux said Mass in private homes before a permanent church existed. In 1849, the permanent church was built in "Uppertown" in St. Anthony. Pierre Bottineau donated the land, and the first church was completed in 1851. By 1855, the German Catholic members had broken with the French and Irish at St. Anthony's, and these breakaway parishioners built St. Boniface in 1858.

Our Lady of Lourdes was organized as the First Universalist Church. In 1887, the French Roman Catholics acquired the church. The staid minimalism was replaced by Catholic flourishes such as a rear building, an apse, a transept and a steeple. Father Alan Moss led the effort to save the church from closure by the archdiocese or eminent domain by surrounding high rises in the 1980s.

The Basilica of St. Mary of Minneapolis, or the Minneapolis Pro-Cathedral, was another creation of French American architect Emmanuel Masqueray. In 1926, it became a minor basilica established by Pope Pius XI. The parish of the Immaculate Conception began as a "shed-church" (1868–73) on the basilica site. Then, the second Immaculate Conception (1873–1914) was constructed. The church was the first Roman Catholic house of worship west of the Mississippi River. Before then, parishioners had to venture across ferries and, later, the toll bridge to the east bank for Mass.

When the Basilica was constructed, Reverend Thomas E. Cullen headed the church. On August 7, 1909, Archbishop John Ireland broke ground. Ireland, a moral crusader, advocated for the "Total Abstinence Movement" that opposed alcohol consumption and attacked "hyphenate Americans," for example, "Irish-Americans."

The Basilica occupied land with an amusing succession of owners. In the 1860s, it was Chandler Hutchins's house and barn. It then passed through several owners before Robert "Fish" Jones snapped up the property. In 1876, he arrived from New York to Minneapolis wearing a top hat and a Prince Albert coat. He had a fish market at 308 Hennepin Avenue in Bridge Square. Later, Jones moved outside the city limits near Minnehaha Falls. The Basilica, years in the making, held an informal opening on May 31, 1914.

St. Mark's Episcopal Cathedral, a small wooden church, originated at Washington Avenue and 2nd Avenue N. In 1863, the church was moved by thirty-three oxen to a lot donated by Franklin Steele and Henry T. Welles to Hennepin Avenue and 4th Street. The church, a meager eighteen by forty-five feet, had to be enlarged. It was relocated several times as property prices increased. Welles's property facing Loring Park was sold. In 1907, ground was broken for the new church. It opened on September 29, 1910. In 1941, St. Mark's became the cathedral for the Diocese of the Episcopal Church.

The Basilica of St. Mary's.

St. Mark's Episcopal Cathedral.

Edwin H. Hewitt (1874–1939) designed the most recent St. Mark's Cathedral. Hewitt attended Hobart College and the University of Minnesota, and he also was a founder of the Minneapolis Institute of Arts. The English Gothic architecture, capped by its massive Gothic tower, was constructed from 1908 to 1911.

Hennepin United Methodist Church showcased the work of architects Hewitt and his son-in-law Edwin Brown. The English Gothic–style church featured a 238-foot spire. In addition, the Dunwoody Institute (1917, 1925) and the former Northwestern National Life Insurance Company (1924) on Loring Park were designed by Hewitt and Brown.

Synagogues celebrated the triumph of immigrant Jews in Minneapolis. The community's growth inspired the scale and splendor of synagogues to bloom.

In 1878, there were only 172 Jewish residents in Minneapolis. Minneapolis's first Jewish congregation was Shaarai Tov, later Temple Israel. Shaarai Tov began in a small wooden building on Marquette Avenue and 2nd Avenue S. In 1888, the temple moved to 10th Street and 5th Avenue S. The temple moved repeatedly due to membership growth and frequent fires. Finally, in 1914, the two-story Smith residence (24th Street and Emerson Avenue) was rented for religious classes. After the 1925 fire, there was discussion about a constructing a new synagogue. Then, in 1928, they relocated to Emerson, and Jacob Liebenberg and Seeman Kaplan were hired. The Twin Cities' most famous movie theater designers served as architects. In 1988, the synagogue hired Marcia Zimmerman, the first female rabbi in Minneapolis.

In 2004, besides Temple Israel, there were two suburban reform congregations. Bet Shalom (1981) began in Hopkins and then moved to Minnetonka. Shir Tikvah (1988) practices liberal Judaism with a scenic location on Minnehaha Parkway. In 1994, the members purchased a Unitarian and Universalist church at 50th Street and Girard Avenue.

Temples closely followed Jewish settlement patterns. Over the years, Jews and temples have moved from Near North and North Minneapolis to south of downtown, Uptown and, finally, to the suburbs of St. Louis Park, Hopkins and Minnetonka.

Explosive economic expansion spurred Minneapolis's enormous growth: between 1880 and 1900, the city expanded from approximately 50,000 to over 200,000 residents. But it wouldn't have occurred without immigration. Historic churches and synagogues were established in locations throughout the city to serve the immigrants' needs.

Eastern European heritage displayed in a Dinkytown entranceway.

Since the 1990s, a new wave of immigrants has arrived in Minneapolis. And they have transformed churches in the city. For example, Mexicans, Central Americans and Ecuadorians have reinvigorated old Roman Catholic churches.

Somali immigrants prayed with less numerous Muslims but have also converted fraternal halls and neglected office space and constructed new buildings for mosques. Like the Christians and Jews who settled before them did, grandiose and more immense houses of worship will soon be constructed in the future.

YOUR GUIDE TO HISTORY

Alliance Française of the Twin Cities
113 1st Street N
Minneapolis, MN 55401
(612) 332-0436
afmsp.org

Alliance Française offers French classes for kids of all ages and adults and gives members access to a wide selection of French films, books and contemporary magazines. It also offers French cooking classes and meets at some of the best restaurants and cocktail bars in town that feature haute cuisine and aperitifs.

Basilica of St. Mary

1600 Hennepin Avenue
Minneapolis, MN 55403
(612) 333-1381
Free

Built in 1914, the Basilica of St. Mary is the first Basilica built in the United States. Year-round, people visit the church both for religious services and to view the building's incredible art and architecture. The Basilica is also home to the Basilica Block Party, a summer music event that draws thousands of people, with the proceeds going toward the upkeep and necessary repairs of the historic building.

Beltrami Park

1111 Summer Street NE
Minneapolis, MN 55413
(612) 230-6400
www.minneapolisparks.org

Beltrami Park is the former site of Maple Hill Cemetery, where the city's Italian immigrant community was primarily interred. In 1947, the park was renamed for Giacomo Constantino Beltrami, an Italian explorer who is credited with being the first European to identify the source of the Mississippi River in 1823.

Hillside Cemetery

2600 19th Avenue NE
Minneapolis, MN 55418
(612) 781-3391
www.washburn-mcreavy.com

Minnesota American Indian Center/Two Rivers Gallery

1530 East Franklin Avenue
Minneapolis, MN 55404
(612) 879-1700
www.maicnet.org

The Minneapolis American Indian Center is one of the oldest in the country, offering a variety of support services for the Native American community. Two Rivers Gallery, located inside the center, provides a space for Native American artists to exhibit their work and offers youth and adult classes in a variety of traditional arts.

Minnesota American Indian Center/Two Rivers Gallery represents the original people of the area. The American Indian Movement (AIM) was founded in North Minneapolis by Clyde Bellecourt and Dennis Banks on July 29, 1968. Both were Ojibwe, the former from the White Earth Reservation, the latter from Leech Lake. The group began fighting employment discrimination cases and tried to end neighborhood discrimination. In 1968, the organization started an AIM patrol to "police the police." As Anton S. Treuer said in *Ojibwe in Minnesota*, "AIM was initially created to deal with Indian urbanization and poverty in Minneapolis."

Norway House

913 East Franklin Avenue
Minneapolis, MN 55404
(612) 871-2211
www.norwayhouse.org
See website for special event prices

The Norway House presents art and film exhibits by contemporary and historic artists from Norway as well as performances by touring musical acts.

Our Lady of Lourdes Catholic Church

One Lourdes Place
Minneapolis, MN 55414
(612) 379-2259
lourdesmpls.org

Built in 1854 by the First Universalist Society and expanded after being purchased by the Catholic Church in 1877, Our Lady of Lourdes is the oldest continuously used church in Minneapolis.

Polish American Cultural Institute of Minnesota (PACIM)

43 Main Street SE, Suite 228
Minneapolis, MN 55414
(612) 378-9291
pacim.org

As a major sponsor of the Twin Cities Polish Festival, the PACIM features ethnic dancing, food, music and cultural exhibits both at the festival and at smaller events around the Twin Cities. Year-round, PACIM's members have access to a library of over five thousand titles in both English and Polish, events and classes that celebrate Polish heritage and culture.

Russian Soul

1624 3rd Street NE
Minneapolis, MN 55413
(612) 465-9309
www.rusculturemn.com

Russian Soul is a nonprofit organization dedicated to the study, preservation and promotion of the Russian language, folk culture and art. Among its offerings are classes in Russian history, folk music, medicine and making traditional costumes for festivals.

St. Anthony's Cemetery

2730 Central Avenue NE
Minneapolis, MN 55418
(763) 537-4184
www.catholic-cemeteries.org

St. Anthony's Cemetery was originally opened as a parish cemetery in 1857 by St. Anthony's Parish. The thirteen-acre cemetery is particularly known for its forest of majestic oak trees.

St. Mark's Episcopal Cathedral

519 Oak Grove Street
Minneapolis, MN 55403
(612) 870-7800
ourcathedral.org

St. Mark's Episcopal Cathedral was opened in 1910. It was designed by parishioner and architect Edwin H. Hewitt. Trained in Europe as well as in the United States, he envisioned a neo-Gothic design, airy, light and warm. Its official designation as Cathedral came in 1941, on the eve of America's entry into World War II. The Cathedral was a focal point of the church's historic 1976 General Convention in Minneapolis, during which women were first officially accepted for ordination to the priesthood.

St. Mary's Cemetery

4403 Chicago Avenue
Minneapolis, MN
(651) 488-8866
www.catholic-cemeteries.org

St. Mary's Cemetery was originally opened as a parish cemetery in 1873 by the Church of the Immaculate Conception, now the Basilica of St. Mary. A focal point of the sixty-five-acre property is the memorial to the firefighters of the City of Minneapolis. Each year, St. Mary's hosts Memorial Day festivities, which include a parade, recognition of veterans of past wars, Mass and refreshments.

Sunset Cemetery
2250 St Anthony Boulevard NE
Minneapolis, MN 55418
(612) 789-3596
www.dignitymemorial.com

Sunset Funeral Home and Sunset Cemetery opened in 1922. One of the property's most recognizable landmarks, the seventy-five-foot Tower of Memories, was built in the 1930s. The twenty-five-tone set of Deagan chimes within its belfry fills the air with music.

Temple Israel Memorial Park Cemetery
4153 3rd Avenue S
Minneapolis, MN 55409
(612) 377-8680
templeisrael.com

Temple Israel Memorial Cemetery is the final resting place for Minneapolis Reform Judaism. The oldest synagogue in the city is now among the ten largest in the United States.

Ukrainian American Community Center
301 Main Street NE
Minneapolis, MN 55413
(612) 379-1956
uaccmn.org

The Ukrainian American Community Center's mission is to promote Ukrainian culture and heritage through activities such as traditional folk dance, music and art exhibits.

Westminster Presbyterian Church

1200 Marquette Ave S
Minneapolis, MN 55403
(612) 332-3421
www.westminstermpls.org

Located in Downtown Minneapolis, Westminster Presbyterian Church first opened its doors in 1897. The massive Gothic building, with its huge stained-glass windows—including its sixteen-foot-wide Nicollet Mall Rose Window, containing over four thousand pieces of leaded glass—is listed in the National Registry of Historic Places.

8

POLITICIANS, POLITICS AND SCANDAL

New England–style town hall democracy was the dream of a significant contingent of settlers in St. Anthony. But in asserting power, these elites developed a system that largely excluded everyone else in government.

In Minneapolis, the city charter—the constitution of the city—created a weak mayor system. Mayoral terms changed in the city charter from one, two and four years. The number of aldermen, later city council members, changed over the years, too. In 1887, there were thirty-nine aldermen. Since the 1950s, the number of aldermen/city council members was consolidated to thirteen.

There were six attempts at home rule between 1898 and 1920. In 1920, a referendum finally passed. With abolitionist roots, St. Anthony, and then Minneapolis, voted Republican from 1860 until 1932, except during the 1912 election, when the city supported Theodore Roosevelt's Bull Moose Party. Rufus J. Baldwin accurately stated in "The History of the City of Minneapolis," "A majority of the people of Minneapolis have always been of the Republican faith. That of the neighboring city of St. Paul have been as decisively Democratic."

In 1896, Minnesota became the fourth state to allow "home rule." The home rule amendment attempted to remedy the city government's responsiveness to the U.S. Constitution and implemented municipal independence to serve the people. It was rejected by city voters in a referendum, repeatedly. In 1900, Minneapolis voters rejected the new charter. The business leaders

Historic downtown Hennepin Avenue.

formed the anti-labor Citizens Alliance. Attempts at creating a new charter failed in 1904, 1906, 1907 and 1913 but finally passed in 1920. But the "weak mayor" system continued. The *Star-Tribune* wrote editorials in support of reforms again in 1948, 1960 and 1963—but all failed. Labor opposed a new charter because of fear of a "dictator mayor." However, the city charter was amended. In 1951, it reduced city council members from twenty-six to thirteen; one member, instead of two, represented each ward.

At city hall, four-term mayor Albert Alonzo "Doc" Ames led the city during the most corrupt period in the history of Minneapolis. In his final term, as Erik Rivenes wrote in "Dirty Doc Ames," he "created a crime syndicate…that would have made Boss Tweed envious."

Doc was the son of Albert Elisha Ames, one of the first physicians in Minnesota. He had served in the Illinois State House of Representatives and the Minnesota Territorial House of Representatives and attended the Minnesota Constitutional Convention (1857). Doc, like his father, graduated from Rush Medical Institution in Chicago. During the Civil War, he served as a surgeon.

Medicine and politics—of an increasingly corrupt manner—were Doc's lifelong endeavors. He served in the Minnesota House of Representatives as an alderman, lost to William D. Washburn (1882) in a congressional bid and ran for governor twice as both Democrat and Republican. In 1888, he was even mentioned as a potential Democratic vice presidential candidate. In 1876, he was elected mayor. In the 1870s, terms were only one year, before extending to a two-year term in 1882 and 1886. He was accused of corruption from the start. But in 1886, he engaged in further vice. He lost the mayoral job to George Pillsbury—the father of the Liquor Patrol Limits (LPL), a system that limited the location of bars and saloons to along the river and downtown until 1974.

In 1884, Mayor George Pillsbury developed a system that lasted for ninety years. Saloons were on both sides of the river, in the Gateway District and St. Anthony, parts of Northeast Minneapolis and Cedar-Riverside. No hard liquor was permitted outside this area. Many sections of the city were permitted to have only neighborhood 3.2 bars. These bars could sell beer with no greater than 3.2 percent alcohol.

Once again, in 1898, Doc ran for mayor, this time as an independent against a competitor who had served as editor of the *Minneapolis Tribune* and *Times*. Doc lost. James Gray succeeded in securing the eight-hour workday. City reforms were made to limit kingmaking by party leadership à la Tammany Hall in New York for the 1900 election. Doc, running as a progressive Republican reformer, defeated John Schlener, his party-backed primary opponent. Then, in the general election, riding the coattails of President William McKinley, Ames was victorious as a Republican for the first time, beating the incumbent Gray and William J. Dean, a Prohibition candidate.

Doc immediately recommenced his corrupt rule as mayor. First, he appointed his brother Fred, sixteen years his junior, as police chief. Then, he cleaned house within the police department, ensuring the allegiance of all members of the force: 105 officers remained, 112 were hired and 105 were fired. Doc Ames used the police force for his own corrupt purposes. Doc's shenanigans went as far as offering Cole Younger a position as police commander after his release from prison in 1901. Younger declined. Doc's vice district in Bridge Square swindled out-of-town businessmen and tourists in "big mitt" scams. A ledger contained records of the money from victims of card games that went to the detective, police chief and mayor.

The deck was stacked against suckers with the big mitt. But the big mitt left a trail of paper behind that led to indictment. The case involved Roman Miex traveling to Michigan, but he stopped in Minneapolis. In a card game, a Minneapolis police detective cheated Miex of $100. Fred Ames and two other police officers were indicted on May 16, 1902. Fred Ames was first acquitted but then given a six-and-a-half-year sentence in the second trial. Meanwhile, Doc was on the lam in West Baden, Indiana, and Louisville, Kentucky.

Then, they lost his trail.

Minneapolis's corruption attracted national attention, most notably that of the famous muckraking journalist Lincoln Steffens. In order to increase circulation, he detailed municipal corruption with bombastic sensational writing for *McClure Magazine*. Simultaneously, in essays about civil vice, he promoted a progressive agenda.

Minneapolis newspaper photographer Edward A. Bromley discovered Doc's trail. He was hiding at his sister-in-law's house in Hancock, New Hampshire. When interviewed, Doc feigned illness—"hereditary insanity"—which he used in his criminal defense.

Doc faced nine indictments, and he was convicted to serve six years at Stillwater. But, in an appeals court, the conviction was overturned.

Doc was on trial three times; they ended in mistrials and no convictions.

Ames returned to medicine, and he died on November 16, 1911. The newspapers were surprisingly evenhanded in their assessment of his seventy years of life—they noted his numerous accomplishments in the obituary but did not leave out the corruption that dominated his last mayoral term. His death was "unexpected," reported both the *Minneapolis Journal* and the *Minneapolis Tribune*.

Steffens published his article in January 1903. In the years since, historians have debunked his narrative with overly arch characters such as the jury foreman Hovey C. Clarke who heroically saved the city from corruption. However, Steffens's descriptions are apt and insightful, if slightly exaggerated, as in the case of Doc: "Ames was sunshine not to the sick and destitute only. To the vicious and the depraved also he was a comfort. If a man was a hard drinker, the good Doctor cheered him with another drink; if he had stolen something, the doctor helped to get him off."

Steffens also assessed the city's historical position based on his research, "And yet Minneapolis was not nearly so bad as St. Louis; police graft is never so universal as boodle."

Minneapolis corruption moved from city hall to the streets following Prohibition, when Isadore "Kid Cann" Blumenfeld built his criminal empire. Kid Cann was a Jew from North Minneapolis who was born in Romania in 1900. His brothers Yiddy and Harry were the brains of his operation. After Prohibition began in 1933, Kid Cann controlled liquor licensing through extortion. In 1945, he opened the Casablanca (later the Gay 90's) to legitimize his business. After Hubert Humphrey kicked Davie "the Jew" Berman out of Minneapolis, Kid Cann cornered the market on questionably corrupt activities.

The corruption continued, as Neal Karlen noted in "Augie's Secret," between the Gateway District and 8th Street and Hennepin Avenue: "Jews controlled vice, liquor, and almost every organized illegal activity in Minneapolis, often protecting their territory with violence." But Karlen points out the *why* behind the Jews' interest in vice: they were "shut out by the city's business and social elites."

In accordance with civic development, prostitution districts set up shop and relocated. Since the first major sources of wealth were lumber and flour milling, prostitutes set up residences to earn money from the elite and working-class customers. Early in the city's history, prostitution concentrated in Bridge Square on 1st Street and on nearby High Street, behind the present-day downtown U.S. Post Office.

From 1870 to 1910, there were three prostitution districts. They were maintained by the Minneapolis police and the city government: the Main Street district in old St. Anthony, the aforementioned 1st Street district and 11th Avenue, just around the corner from Washington Avenue.

The Gay 90's.

The Sisterhood of Bethany, organized by Charlotte O. Van Cleve and Harriet R. Walker, opposed prostitution and supported the abused women. The group was Protestant and worked with the church to help prostitutes, condemning the city's system of fining but not improving the lives of the prostitutes. The *Minneapolis Journal* headline on July 5, 1906, read, "New Deadline on Red Light District." An August 1 deadline to close the red-light district was declared.

The infamous Barker-Karpis gang robbed the 2nd Northwestern National Bank and Trust Company on March 29, 1932. The gang struck again on December 16—this time resulting in fatalities. The bank robbery of the Third Northwestern National Bank (430 East Hennepin Avenue) was a dangerous and risky crime committed in the afternoon. Moreover, the bank was located at a busy intersection on a triangular lot with a streetcar line where Hennepin and Central Avenues meet. In "John Dillinger Slept Here:

A Crooks Tour of Crime and Corruption in St. Paul," Paul Maccabee called the crime "among the most violent" by the gang. Armed with machine guns and .45 caliber automatics, Fred and Doc Barker, Alvin "Creepy" Karpis, Verne Miller, Jess Doyle and others robbed the bank. Before the robbery, Karpis loaned $4,000, while Fred Barker kicked in $6,500, to the Ralph Van Lear mayoral campaign.

Two Minneapolis policemen—Ira Evans and Leo Gorski—were killed during the gang's escape. Later, the gang had to change a flat tire near Como Park as they prepared for their "switch car"—a Lincoln was exchanged for a less conspicuous Chevy—and the son of Swedish immigrants, Oscar Erickson, was killed. In the wrong place at the wrong time, he was with his friend Arthur Zachman, who was riding in the same vehicle.

Criminals continued to find home in the city. John Dillinger lived briefly in South Minneapolis with his girlfriend Evelyn Frechette in 1930. But not with the notoriety of St. Paul—especially during the (John) O'Conner layover agreement that lasted from 1900 to 1935 under three conditions: 1) check in with the police, 2) pay all bribes 3) commit no major crimes in the city.

Floyd B. Olson (1891–1936) was a political leader with a bright future. As George A. Mayer said in *The Political Career of Floyd B. Olson*, "When a pancreatic cancer abruptly cut short the career of Floyd B. Olson on the eve of the 1936 election, his political career was definitely in the ascendant that not even the presidency seemed beyond his reach." He grew up in North Minneapolis, and as a shabbos goy, he lit candles and stoves for Jews on Fridays. He was the only son of Swedish immigrants and attended university and eventually law school at night. In the 1920s, as county attorney, he prosecuted seven Minneapolis aldermen who received kickbacks from local businessmen. Olson exposed graft and sent four aldermen to prison in 1929. Olson also collaborated with Thomas J. Dillon of the *Tribune* in his investigation.

During that epoch, corruption was so widespread that Mayor George E. Leach and Police Chief Frank Brunskill were tied to local underworld characters. Olson's opposition went beyond protecting civil liberties through "prior restraint" of the vilest in the case of Jay Near, the editor of the sensationalistic and virulent antisemitic *Saturday Press*. In the 1920s, Near's paper attacked "Jewish hoodlums."

In 1930, Olson was elected as Farmer-Labor governor of Minnesota. William E. Lass said in *Minnesota: A History*, "The stock market plunge and subsequent depression, which embarrassed the old order in both Washington and St. Paul, opened the way for the emergence of one of

Floyd B. Olson.

the most colorful and controversial figures in Minnesota's history—Floyd B. Olson. As Minnesota's New Deal governor, Olson attracted national attention as a speaker, as an advocate of change, and…even presidential candidate." The Farmer-Labor Party had roots in a long tradition of third parties in Minnesota. Labor was involved in the Anti-Monopoly Party, later the Greenback Party, and finally backed the Populist Party. But by 1900, the Populist Party had moved to the Non-Partisan League and the Farmer-Labor Party, which the communists repeatedly tried to take over and transform into a radical party. After World War I and the Red Scare, communists went underground as the Workers Party in 1919. And this was the backdrop when Olson was elected. The Farmer-Labor Party won three governorships and four U.S. Senate races between 1923 and 1939. Minneapolis was an "open shop" town in the 1930s

Arthur Naftalin—future mayor of Minneapolis from 1960 to 1966—in his doctoral thesis for the University of Minnesota, "A History of the Farmer Labor Party of Minnesota," (1948) described the political milieu that Olson entered at the onset of the Depression: "It was perhaps inevitable in the development of the Farmer-Labor Party that, once it had acquired a measure of power and its candidates had begun to taste success at the polls, the driving force behind the movement should experience a shift from idealism to expediency." Olson was compared to John A. Johnson; both were Scandinavians of humble backgrounds and gifted speakers who died too early.

On May 16, 1934, the teamsters went on strike. On May 22, the striking truckers from the General Drivers Union, the Teamsters Local 574, fought with the Citizens Alliance, backed by the police. The teamsters included avowed "Trotyskyist Communists" who were used by Citizens Alliance for propaganda purposes conflated with antisemitism because of Eastern European Jews involvement in communism. The Citizens Alliance claimed the entire organization was a "red menace."

On July 16, the second strike began, and it was much worse. As Naftalin said, "The violence that followed during the next week made the May outbreak appear like a preliminary skirmish." On July 20, 1934, Police Chief Mike Johannes known as "Bloody Mike"—ordered the police to fire to get the trucks through. In the aftermath, sixty-seven were wounded and two killed, including strikers and bystanders.

Truck drivers were permitted back on the job on July 26. Olson called up the National Guard. On August 5, the Citizens Alliance exploited the permit system to move goods. The strike resumed.

Employers called the strikers "communists." Olson disagreed in a letter, and martial law was declared in Minneapolis. If there was no settlement by midnight of August 5, 1934, all trucks would stop, and no special permits were allowed. Finally, the employers agreed to settlement on August 21, 1934. Olson stepped in, Naftalin said, and "the agreement was a modest, but definite, victory for the workers; they won a minimum wage, reinstatement of all strikers without discrimination, arbitration of further wage disputes, seniority in hiring and layoffs, and, most important of all, recognition of the union."

Olson was flexible, despite his ideology. He, wisely, did not foist socialism into a powder keg of a situation but instead worked pragmatically for a solution. However, his efforts led to the Farmer-Labor Party losing political support. He worked with Franklin Delano Roosevelt and did not promote a third party nationally while a Farmer-Labor member. In 1936, he ran for U.S. Senate but died of cancer.

Another reformer who battled city corruption was Hubert H. Humphrey. Lass described him as the "central figure in Minneapolis politics for three decades." He began his political career after practicing pharmacy. He

Hubert H. Humphrey statue at city hall.

was from South Dakota and a New Deal Democrat. He ousted the DFL communists, championed civil rights and united the Democrats and Olson's Farmer-Labor Party. In 1945, he was elected mayor of Minneapolis and reelected for a second term in 1947. The DFL was created in April 1944 when the weaker Democratic Party formed with the Farmer-Labor Party, the DFL Party. In 1946, the first Urban Fair Employment Practices Commission was created. Humphrey was elected to the U.S. Senate and served from 1949 to 1964 and in 1970. He died in 1978.

Humphrey's civil rights agenda responded to social inequity and racism. In 1946, Carey McWilliams wrote for the periodical *Common Ground*, stingingly pointing out racism in the city. This left a bitter taste in Humphrey's mouth, and he established

Fair Employment Practices (FEPC) to combat discrimination in the workplace against Jews, African Americans and American Indians. In *Minneapolis in the Twentieth Century*, Iric Nathanson described the city during this time: "In Minneapolis, a tightly-knit Anglo-Saxon Protestant elite with New England roots controlled the local economy and erected informal barriers to participation by outsiders."

Humphrey received national attention at the 1948 Democratic National Convention, an in the 1950s, he was mentioned as a possible candidate for president. As President Lyndon Baines Johnson's vice president, he was tied to his politics in Vietnam, however. Walter Mondale was appointed to serve Humphrey's Senate term. Humphrey, a first ballot nominee at the 1968 Democratic National Convention in Chicago, lost the election to Richard M. Nixon.

In 1968, Humphrey's loss to Nixon ended the reign of the party bosses. Selecting the Democratic Party presidential candidate in smoked-filled rooms, handpicked by party bosses, was rebuked by the electoral defeat of Senator Humphrey. Thereafter, the Democratic National Convention relied on the caucuses and primaries to endorse a candidate in the federal presidential election.

Art Naftalin reappeared, decades later, not as political scientist, but as politician. The riot in North Minneapolis brought Governor Karl Rolvaag and Mayor Naftalin to the table to deal with the unrest on the streets. In the *Minneapolis Tribune* account, the headlines describe the action taken after the event: "Negroes' Grievances Heard" and "Governor, Mayor Promise Jobs." The mayor promised sixty jobs while Steven M. Crawford, a spokesman for African Americans in the area, announced, "If something isn't done about our wants, Plymouth's [Avenue] going to burn!" to a cheering crowd.

During the riot, Naftalin phoned Harry Davis on July 20, 1967. Dedicated to improving race relations, Davis said that an African American was shot at Wayne's Bar. Stores were afire from Plymouth Avenue to Penn Avenue and Humboldt Avenue while eight blocks were damaged. The businesses from Penn Avenue to Humboldt Avenue burned. In *North Side Memories*, Rabbi Kassel Abelson said of racial violence, "With the riots, Jews no longer felt safe coming to the neighborhood."

Charles Stenvig capitalized on social disarray as the "law and order" candidate. In 1967, Stenvig was the head of the Minneapolis Police Federation. Then, two years later, he was elected mayor of Minneapolis on a law and order platform. In 1971, Stenvig defeated Harry Davis. Future mayor Sharon Sayles Belton, decades later, was told by Davis that she would one day become mayor. In 1973, Al Hofstede won, only to be defeated by Stenvig in the 1975 election. But Hofstede was reelected in 1977. During the 1970s, the mayors seesawed like prizefighters with a punch and then a counterpunch. Hofstede won in 1973. Stenvig returned in 1976. But Hofstede was back again in 1978–79.

Donald M. Fraser was a University of Minnesota law student who turned to politics. His father, Everett, was the dean of the law school. During World War II, Donald served for one year in the U.S. Navy. In 1954, he was elected to the state senate. In 1962, he defeated Republican U.S. Representative Walter Judd, and he served sixteen years in the U.S. Congress. In 1978, Fraser sought higher office in the U.S. Senate, but he lost to Bob Short in the Democratic primary. He was elected Minneapolis mayor in 1979 and served the last two-year mayoral term. In 1981, Fraser was elected to a four-year term and again in 1985 and 1989. As of this writing, he was Minneapolis's longest-serving mayor, in office until 1993. He passed away on June 2, 2019.

Donald and his wife, Arvonne, were an important team in the civic life of Minneapolis. A senior fellow at the Hubert H. Humphrey School of Public Affairs, Arvonne served on the Marcy-Holmes Neighborhood Association. She also wrote the memoir *She's No Lady: Politics, Family, and International Feminism*. Arvonne died on August 7, 2018.

DFL senator Allan Spear was "a nationally celebrated gay rights icon," said Joshua Preston in *Minnesota History Magazine*. In 1972, he first won election to the Minnesota State Senate. He served with distinction until 2000. But he did not come out until December 9, 1974. The announcement was announced in the *Minneapolis Star* newspaper. He was inspired by Massachusetts state representative Elaine Noble, who was elected in 1974—the first openly gay or lesbian representative elected to a state legislature. Due to Spear's efforts, Minnesota became the eighth state to include gays and lesbians in its human rights act—and the first to include transgender individuals. The bill was cosponsored by Representative Karen Clark, a nurse and out lesbian elected in 1980.

The University of Minnesota, where Spear taught, has become a national leader in LGBT studies with the world-renowned Tretter Collection. It is stored at the Elmer L. Andersen Library at the University of Minnesota. The Jean Nickolaus Tretter Collection in Gay, Lesbian, Bisexual, and Transgender Studies at the University of Minnesota is, as Stewart Van Cleve said in his book, "one of the most comprehensive

Former Milwaukee Road Depot turned hotel.

archives of international queer history in the world." Tretter's donation of his extensive collection was at first met with trepidation by Republican Governor Elmer Andersen and his namesake library. However, Andersen was won over and put up much of the money for the collection's inclusion in the library.

In 1973, the first Twin Cities Pride Parade was held. In 1982, there was "the great split" between gays and lesbians, with the latter holding events at Powderhorn Park and the former at Loring Park. In 1982, Minneapolis closed its streets during a pride parade for the first time. In protest, because of discrimination, the parade was in St. Paul once, in 1983. It was not until 1996 that the pride parade received corporate funding.

Brian Coyle was on the Minneapolis City Council Sixth Ward from 1983 until 1991. He represented Cedar-Riverside as an openly gay city council member. At age forty-seven, he died from AIDS on August 23, 1991. His sister, Kathy, said he was "a leader who was gay" not a "gay leader." President of the city council and later mayor of Minneapolis Sharon Sayles Belton said, "Brian Coyle was a strong advocate for the gay and lesbian and low-income communities of the city of Minneapolis." Coyle had grown up in Moorhead, Minnesota, as a rabid Republican before attending the University of Minnesota, where he became a progressive DFL supporter. After his death, flags were flown at half-staff at Minneapolis City Hall for a week.

YOUR GUIDE TO HISTORY

Federal Reserve Bank of Minneapolis
90 Hennepin Avenue
Minneapolis, MN 55401
(612) 204-5000
www.minneapolisfed.org

The Federal Reserve Bank of Minneapolis was incorporated on May 18, 1914, one of twelve district banks established after the signing of the Federal Reserve Act by President Woodrow Wilson on December 23, 1913.

Minneapolis City Hall and Hennepin County Courthouse
350 5th Street S
Minneapolis, MN 55415
(612) 596-9512
www.municipalbuildingcommission.org

The Minneapolis City Hall and Hennepin County Courthouse is a historic venue surrounded by stained-glass windows and carved Italian marble, now managed by the Municipal Building Commission and used mostly for rental space for events and weddings.

Twin Cities PRIDE Parade
Loring Park
1382 Willow Street
Minneapolis, MN 55403
(612) 255-3260
tcpride.org

The Twin Cities PRIDE Parade and festival celebrates LGBTQ+ community in the Twin Cities. Hundreds of exhibit booths and food venders fill Loring Park for the event, while multiple stages feature a variety of live entertainment.

9

NEWSPAPERS, TV STATIONS, RADIO STATIONS

Newspapers were organized with the advent of Minnesota Territory. The first issue of the *Minnesota Pioneer* was edited and published by New Hampshire native James Madison Goodhue on April 28, 1849. The paper was four page and six columns, the first of eighty-nine territorial newspapers from 1849 to 1858.

Newspapers were partisan, with distinct political leanings, in the nineteenth century. This strongly affected the *how* and *why* of reporting and the narrative of events presented. Thus, bias, especially partisan platform-based bias, was expected. During this time, papers viewed events through specific lenses, and each paper presented stories with a particular, and often predictable, perspective.

The *Saint Anthony Express* originated when Elmer Tyler, a tailor, convinced Isaac Atwater to edit his weekly newspaper in April 1851. It was the seventh in the state of Minnesota but the first outside of St. Paul. The weekly paper was first issued on May 31, 1851. In 1852, George D. Bowman of Wilkes-Barre, Pennsylvania, became the editor, and he later served in the same position at another local paper, the *Atlas*. The four-page and seven column *St. Anthony Express* was of a Whig political bent. However, politics could not prevent the papers' demise. The paper closed permanently with the Civil War on the horizon on April 21, 1860.

The *Minnesota Republican* was edited by Reverend Charles G. Ames in St. Anthony, and the first issue appeared on October 5, 1854. George S. Hage stated in *Newspapers on the Minnesota Frontier*, "It was the first newspaper in the Northwest and perhaps the country to carry the name of the emerging political party." The antislavery leaders of St. Anthony financed the paper: John W. North, William R. Marshall and Dr. Vickers Fell. It was renamed the *Minnesota State News* in 1859 and edited by W.A. Croffutt. In 1863, it was sold to the William S. King and merged with the *Atlas*. In 1851, the *Minnesotian* was a four-page and seven-column Whig partisan paper that served St. Paul and Bridge Square.

The *Northwestern Democrat* (1853–56) was established by George Prescott in St. Anthony. It was later purchased by Joel Bassett and published in both St. Anthony and Minneapolis. The paper was issued for only a few months. In September 1858, the paper was purchased by C.H. Pettit and John G. Williams, who later started

KFAI radio.

the *Minneapolis Journal*. Alexander Russell changed the *Minnesota Democrat*'s (1856) name to the *Minneapolis Gazette* (1857). The *Minneapolis Gazette* was absorbed by the *Minneapolis Journal* in 1858. William S. King opened the *Atlas* in 1859, and the paper was published until 1867, when it became the *Minneapolis Daily Tribune*. William D. Washburn and Dorilus Morrison arranged the merger. The first day of publication was May 25, 1867. The paper briefly battled the *Minneapolis Daily Chronicle*, the paper supported by Colonel John H. Stevens. According to Bradley Morison, in *Sunlight on Your Doorstep*, Stevens "mourned" the merger that joined the paper with *Atlas* but wanted peace for the Republican Party without infighting between partisan newspapers.

Minneapolis's newspaper row was located on 4th Street between Nicollet Avenue and 1st Avenue S (present-day Marquette Avenue S) in the late nineteenth and early twentieth centuries. Over the years, the newspapers included the *Minneapolis Penny Press*, the *Minneapolis Journal*, the *Minneapolis Times* and the *Minneapolis* Tribune, plus offices for the *St. Paul Globe* and the *St. Paul Pioneer Press.*

William McNally, William Murphy's nephew, spoke of the "glamour and romance" of newspaper row. He was the architect of the merger of the *Star* and *Tribune*. Morison's book said, "This was Newspaper Row, and for many of us it was the center of the universe in those now-misty days when Babe

John H. Stevens at the Stevens House.

Ruth and Bill Tilden and Floyd B. Olson and Col. Charles A. Lindbergh and the Great Depression and the New Deal and the trial of Leopold and Loeb and the bloody truck drivers' strike were all part of an exciting and often tragic news panorama."

The *Star Tribune* is Minneapolis longest-running newspaper, under various names, locations and forms. From its origin, it was intended to be the city's leading newspaper. And the paper achieved its stated goal through the backing of the city's leading citizens, acquisitions and mergers.

Colonel William S. King—an honorific—arrived in Minneapolis in 1858 from New York. A crucial Minneapolis booster and organizer of contentious state fairs that pitted the Twin Cities against each other, he served in Congress in 1875. King founded the *State Atlas*, a radical Republican newspaper that he merged with the *Minneapolis Tribune* in 1867. Investors W.D. Washburn and Dorilus Morrison, the first mayor of Minneapolis, published the paper on February 19, 1867. At that time, Minneapolis was a city of a mere seven thousand, without city water, a hospital or a fire department.

In the early years, the *Tribune* went through numerous ownership changes. One unusual newspaper partnership was the brief merger with the *Pioneer Press* in 1876. It was referred to as the *Dual City Pioneer-Press and Tribune*, but the masthead read *Pioneer-Press and Tribune*. The paper published a combined Minneapolis and St. Paul edition—it failed. But that was not the opinion of the editorial titled "Journalistic Evolution," which compared the newspaper to Darwinism's survival of the fittest in the first issue on May 2, 1876.

Just before the turn of the century, the primary competitors of the *Minneapolis Tribune* were the *Minneapolis Times*, with its morning and Sunday paper, and the *St. Paul Pioneer Press*. In 1899, the daily paper circulation numbers were: *Minneapolis Tribune*, 44,410; *Evening Journal*, 43,587; and *Minneapolis Times*, 29,636.

The first paper of the consolidated *Minneapolis Star-Tribune* had a surprisingly radical history. The *Minneapolis Star* was financed by the Non-Partisan League in 1920. The progressive organization led an "agrarian revolt" in North Dakota that spread through the upper Midwest. The organization espoused state socialism, and the paper was considered "bush league" in its early years of publication but established headquarters in a four-story building on 6th Avenue (now Portland Avenue) and 5th Street, which became part of the longtime *Star-Tribune* complex.

In 1924, the *Star* went into receivership. The paper was purchased by A.B. Frizell, publisher, and John Thompson, a former executive at the *New York Times*. In 1935, the Cowles family purchased the *Star*. Gardner Cowles Sr. owned the

Des Moines Register—before that, he was a banker. John Cowles's leadership turned the paper around with management and editing improvements and challenged the *Tribune* and *Journal*. By 1936, the *Tribune*'s circulation challenged the *Journal* and the *Evening Tribune*. As a result, the *Journal* was acquired by the *Star* in 1939, creating the *Star-Journal*. On May 1, 1941, the *Tribune* merged with the *Star-Journal* and became the *Star and Tribune*. In six years, John Cowles had transformed the landscape of journalism in Minneapolis. Cowles would serve as publisher, with his son John Jr. as the editor. The paper eliminated writers' bias and became nonpartisan, though it continued to support Republican candidates until the 1964 presidential election, when the editorial staff backed Lyndon B. Johnson over Barry Goldwater.

After sixty-one years, the *Minneapolis Star* closed on April 2, 1982. The staff of the *Minneapolis Star* and *Tribune* was no longer separated. *Star* staffers were either reassigned at the *Tribune* or laid off. The *Minneapolis Star Tribune* continued to publish morning and evening editions.

In Minneapolis, foreign-language papers were primarily Scandinavian and German. The Swedish and Norwegian press was in a constant state of flux; several papers came and went only to be replaced.

Norwegian newspapers included *Budstikken* (the *Messenger*), 1873–1894. The paper merged with *Faedrelandet og Emigranten* (the *Fatherland and the Emigrant*) to form the *Minneapolis Tidende* (*Times*) Norwegian daily. It continued into the 1930s. Other papers included *Nordish Folkebladet* (*People's Paper*), organized in Rochester in 1868. It moved to Minneapolis in 1969. *Nye Normanden* (*New Norseman*) was printed from 1894 to 1922. In addition, journals existed for women, farming and families.

Odd S. Lovoll wrote in the article "Norwegian Newspapers in America: Connecting Norway and the New Land," that "Minneapolis, as the metropolis of the Upper Midwest, was obviously an attractive location for Norwegian American journalism." In 1886, the editor and publisher of *Faedrelandet og Emigranten*, Ferdinand Husher, moved from La Crosse, Wisconsin, to Minneapolis to compete with Minneapolis's Norwegian newspapers.

With the exception of Chicago, Minneapolis led the nation with the most Swedish newspapers. Ebbe Westergren, in "Snoose Boulevard and the Golden Mile" (2006), said that the "Golden Era" of Swedish language publications was 1905 to 1915. This was the peak period of Swedish as a primary language in Minneapolis.

The most well known was Swan Turnblad's *Svenska Amerikanska Posten* (SAP). Nils William Olsson and Lawrence G. Hammerstrom, in "Swedes in the Twin Cities," described him: "Swan Turnblad typified the alert, industrious, and clever Swedish newcomer who arrived in the United States with little money but by dint of pluck, ability, and industry was able to rise from his Swedish peasant background and eventually reach a pinnacle of material success."

Swan Turnblad was born Sven Johan Olofsson but occasionally used the patronymic Månsson. His half brother had settled in Vasa, in Goodhue County, and took the surname Turnblad. Young Swan arrived with his father and was involved in printing a book of arithmetic. Then he relocated to Minneapolis, the new Swedish boomtown, in 1879, where he simultaneously was involved in printing and the temperance movement. With great foresight, he launched the *SAP* in March 1883, just as the greatest influx of Swedes—many speaking little English—arrived.

After amassing a small fortune, Turnblad dreamed of building a mansion. Unfortunately, for him, his first location was the last prestigious lot at modern-day Loring Park. It was purchased for $25,000 in 1899. His property acquisition was opposed by the Minneapolis Park Board and eventually adjudicated by the Minnesota Supreme Court—he lost. Later, he selected the Park Avenue site.

An important and enduring Jewish newspaper began in Minneapolis: The *American Jewish World*. It was first published in 1914 by Rabbi Samuel Dienard of Shaarai Tov, now Temple Israel. The weekly newspaper bridged the gap

American Swedish Institute.

WCCO Television.

WCCO Radio.

between German and eastern European Jews. Today, the paper continues in suburban St. Louis Park.

African American newspapers have had a historical significance in Minneapolis's history. Serving a readership whose stories were not covered or misrepresented, the papers are community-based and give voice to those who are discriminated against. J.Q. Adams edited the *Western Appeal*, based in St. Paul. However, Minneapolis soon followed with many papers of its own. Most papers lasted for less than a couple years. The Minneapolis papers included, the *Twin Cities American*, later the *Afro-American Advance*; the *Northwestern Vine*, edited by D.E. Butler and Frederick D. McCracken; the *Minneapolis Observer*, edited by A.G. Plummer; and the *Minneapolis Messenger*, edited by C.S. Smith.

Cecil E. Newman was a Pullman porter and a newspaper editor. He served as a community leader for decades after arriving in Minneapolis in 1922. In 1934, he founded, edited and published the *Minneapolis Spokesman*. First published in a Southeast Minneapolis barbershop, Newman's paper emphasized African American participation in politics and organized protests and pickets against discrimination. Newman, the social activist, not only wrote about politics but also participated in political action to advance his community. He was involved in the NAACP and the Urban League.

YOUR GUIDE TO HISTORY

City Pages
650 3rd Avenue S, Suite 1300
Minneapolis, MN 55488
(612) 372-3700
www.citypages.com

The free alternative weekly began as *Sweet Potato* in 1979. The Twin Cities paper has undergone several ownership changes in the past decades. The *Minneapolis Star Tribune* owns the free weekly today, but it has not lost its focus on local arts, entertainment, food and investigative reporting.

KFAI
1808 Riverside Avenue
Minneapolis, MN 55454
(612) 341-3144
Kfai.org

Since 1978, KFAI has been a volunteer-based community radio station broadcasting news, arts and entertainment programming for an audience of diverse racial, social and economic backgrounds, with a stated goal of providing a voice for people ignored or misrepresented by mainstream media.

KMOJ

2123 West Broadway Suite 200
Minneapolis, MN 55411
(612) 377-0594
kmojfm.com

Founded in 1976, KMOJ's organizational vision is to develop communities of color with information and education through, television, radio and print journalism.

KUOM, University of Minnesota—Twin Cities

610 Rarig Center
330 21st Avenue S
Minneapolis, MN 55455-4405
(612) 625-3500
www.radiok.org

Radio K, KUOM, is the award-winning student-run radio station of the University of Minnesota and offers an eclectic combination of independent rock music. The station showcases insightful examinations of music genres from punk and metal to local music and lives up to the motto "Real College Radio."

WCCO

625 2nd Avenue S
Minneapolis, MN 55402
(612) 370-0611
www.wccoradio.radio.com

WCCO Radio began as WLAG in 1922. In 1923, the call letters were changed to WCCO for Washburn Crosby Company, reflecting new ownership. WCCO hawked the company's wares, namely Betty Crocker's products, to housewives. "The Good Neighbor" was the fifty-thousand-watt radio home of Minnesota Twins baseball from the team's inaugural season in 1961 until 2006. For the 2018 season, the Twins returned to WCCO.

Minnesota Daily

2221 University Ave SE, Suite 450
Minneapolis, MN 55414
(612) 435-5657
www.mndaily.com

In 1877, forty-one students at the U of M began publishing a monthly literary magazine, the *Ariel*, in hopes of providing students a forum to express themselves as well as inform the public on happenings at the university. In 1990, *Ariel* became a daily in newspaper format, and was renamed the *Minnesota Daily*. After a few months of a daily printing schedule, the *Minnesota Daily* combined with the *Minnesota Daily News*, another competitor within the campus community. Over the years, the *Minnesota Daily* has reported on many big events both on and off campus, from the Vietnam War to the women's suffrage movement and campus riots.

Northeaster

2844 Johnson Street NE
Minneapolis, MN 55418
(612) 788-9003
mynortheaster.com

Founded in 1981, the *Northeaster* covers news and events pertaining to Northeast Minneapolis. It's delivered to homes within Northeast Minneapolis and can be found in the free newspaper rack in most stores and businesses throughout the community.

Southside Pride

3200 Chicago Avenue
Minneapolis, MN 55407
(612) 822-4662
southsidepride.com

Southside Pride is a free monthly newspaper operated in and distributed throughout South Minneapolis. The total circulation per month is 46,500, making *Southside Pride* the largest community newspaper in the Twin Cities.

In 2008, Ed Felien published *Take the Streets!*, a radical publication about the University of Minnesota students during the national protest of the mining of Haiphong Harbor and bombing Hanoi in 1972. The book offers a glimpse into historical perspective of the Nixon, the Vietnam War and college resistance.

Southwest Journal

1115 Hennepin Avenue
Minneapolis, MN 55403
www.southwestjournal.com

In 1990, Janis Hall and Terry Gahan launched the *Southwest Journal* in their Linden Hills home, expanding their paper's reach to cover the news and interests for the twenty neighborhoods that make up Southwest Minneapolis. The free newspaper is delivered to over four thousand area homes and businesses every two weeks.

Star Tribune

650 3rd Avenue S Suite 1300
Minneapolis, MN 55488
(612) 673-4000
Startribune.com

A thorough history of the *Star Tribune* is described in this chapter.

10

HISTORY OF SPORTS

NINETEENTH CENTURY TO PRESENT

In the 1850s, St. Anthony and Minneapolis commenced institutions that transferred practices from the East Coast, including the favorite sporting events of the time: horseracing, hiking and nature observation, hunting and fishing. Germans also transplanted the Turnverein, popular exercise and gymnastics organizations. The *Minneapolis Daily Tribune* described sports in Minneapolis on June 22, 1867: "The beautiful weather of the past few days has started the 'sports' into activity, and races, shooting-matches, games of ball and sculling parties are the order of the day."

Despite Minneapolis's harsh winters, bicycling has undergone several crazes. In 1896, the Minneapolis Cycle Path Association (MCPA) constructed the first two bikeways with access to Lake Harriet and Lake Minnetonka. By 1897, there were twenty-eight miles of bike paths. But the first bike craze ended by the early 1900s. Bike riders were replaced by streetcar riders and automobiles drivers.

By 1899, biking had fallen out of fashion. But some continued to ride. Riding for pleasure declined while others continued using the conveyance for transportation. Ross D. Petty wrote about city statistics on "Bicycling in Minneapolis in the Early 20th Century" in *Minnesota History Magazine*. In 1900, fifty-cent bike tags were mandated for riding to maintain deteriorating bike lanes and paths. In that year, there were forty thousand bikes in Minneapolis, but only sixteen to seventeen thousand tags were sold. The Minneapolis Cycle Path Association members paid for path building and repair, including a one-dollar tag on paths around the Chain of Lakes.

Bikeway/pedestrian link between University of Minnesota and Downtown Minneapolis.

In the 1970s, bike lanes reappeared in the city. Biking in the city was sometimes based on fads, but this was not the case with the dramatic number of both cyclists and amenities in the twenty-first century. In 2010, Minneapolis was ranked as the number-one bike-friendly city in *Bicycling* magazine. In 2010, "Nice Ride"—a bike-sharing program—began in Minneapolis.

In the early twentieth century, horseracing was a favorite spectator sport. As Minneapolis developed, driving clubs developed around racing and recreational carriage riding.

The Minnehaha Driving Park, owned by Robert "Fish" Jones, was a harness track. Established in 1888 for $50,000, the one-mile oval-shaped racing track was completed. The jockeys rode on sulkies, two-wheeled horse carts. The driving park occupied sixty acres of land located between 36th to 37th and Minnehaha to 42nd Avenue. In 1889, the driving park opened. It drew crowds of six to seven thousand attendees regularly, but it declared bankruptcy in 1895. With the financial help of Marion Savage, the park reopened in 1901. But after the 1902 season, the park closed abruptly.

In the early twentieth century, America and Minneapolis loved boxing. But the sport was frequently unpermitted because of municipal and state regulations. For twelve years, boxing was banned in Minneapolis, but the ban was challenged by Doc Ames. And, finally, the boxing ban was upheld by Governor Samuel Van Sant. That did not stop promoters, however, from violating the decision.

Ben Brochin flatly states the financial possibilities of boxing in *North Side Memories*: "Another means of income for a lot of the young Jewish men." Pugilism was everywhere at the turn of the twentieth century. For example, the *Minneapolis Tribune* featured an article about a prize fight in Maple Hill Cemetery with spectators sitting on tombstones with four rounds between boxers named Swanson and Hopper on July 8, 1905. W. Harry Davis summed up the position of the sport in *Overcoming*: "It's hard to appreciate today how popular boxing was in America in the 1930s. There were fewer sports for sportswriters to cover and fans to follow. Basketball was in its infancy. Hockey was purely local fascination, bigger in northern Minnesota than in the Twin Cities. Football was dominated by the college rather than the professional game. Baseball was called the nation's pastime, but the big leagues were centered on the East Coast. Boxing got a lot of attention on the sports pages." The sport was omnipresent, so much so that high school boxing teams was common in the early twentieth century.

According to local lore, in 1895, Lewis Rober hand-sewed a leather ball in the Southeast Minneapolis fire station and called it a "kitten ball." Kittenball was also called "sissy ball." By 1925, "diamond ball" had been adopted as the preferred name, and after 1934, it became softball. Sexism often stopped young women from playing sports. Still, trailblazers like Frances Kidd played slow-pitch softball on girls' teams at Pillsbury Settlement House in the 1910s and 1920s.

In 1952, women were banned from men's teams by the National Association of Baseball. Ann Enke wrote in the *Minnesota History Magazine* article "Pioneers, Players, and Politics: Women's Softball in Minneapolis," "Leaders of black recreation programs promoted concepts of womanhood that included competitiveness, self-reliance, confidence, strength, and tomboyishness." And to prove the point, Phyllis Wheatley Settlement House sponsored African American girls' teams.

African American baseball included the Minneapolis Keystones, a barnstorming team, during the dead ball era. In 1876, the Unions were another early Minneapolis African American team.

Minnesota and Minneapolis quickly embraced a love of baseball, as Atkins noted in *Creating Minneapolis*: "Baseball flourished in Minnesota in the

1870s and proved a wonderful diversion." As early as the 1850s, there was baseball in Minnesota. However, the early version was unlike today's game. Games were high-scoring affairs; for example, the North Star Club from St. Paul defeated the Minneapolis team 56–26.

Later, in the nineteenth century, the Minneapolis Millers presented a brand of baseball with greater similarities to the modern game. Before the emergence of college sports, the Millers were the only team game in town. But, in the first years, following a national trend in the halcyon days of the sport, the team was without a consistent moniker. For example, in the first years, the team was sometimes called the "Reds." But in 1884, the Millers stuck. The Northwestern League also included teams from Wisconsin, Michigan, Illinois and Indiana.

In 1902, the American Association formed with both the Millers and St. Paul Saints. Typical for that time before the arrival of the Minnesota Twins was the Minneapolis and St. Paul split doubleheaders; a home game would be played in one of the Twin Cities in the morning and in the other city in the afternoon.

Nicollet Field hosted many historic firsts. General Mills unveiled the first advertisement for Wheaties "the Breakfast of Champions" at the stadium, while the legendary "Sultan of Swat" Babe Ruth ventured to Minneapolis. "The Bambino" played an exhibition game with the Minneapolis Police team in 1935. For decades, Sunday blue laws affected Millers games until state law was amended in 1909. The Millers were forced by these laws to play Sunday matinee games at the Minnehaha Driving Park—even after it closed for the 1909 season. Later, double-headers were concluded at 6:00 p.m. sharp; finally, the law was repealed in 1941.

During the Millers' time in Minneapolis, they had fifteen players inducted in the National Baseball Hall of Fame in Cooperstown, New York. Moreover, the team fielded players such as Joe "Unser Choe" Hauser. He was acquired from Baltimore of the International League and set a record with sixty-nine home runs into the short band box at Nicollet Park in 1933. His record stood until the late 1990s "steroid era." Ted Williams was a Miller during the 1938 season. The mercurially tempered purest hitter in major league history won the American Association Triple Crown before joining the Boston Red Sox and serving during World War II. Hall of Fame knuckle-baller Hoyt Wilhelm spent the 1950 season with the Millers. In the spring of 1951, another player enshrined in Cooperstown amazed fans with his dazzling defense and five-tool exploits before joining the New York Giants and winning the Rookie of the Year—Willie Mays.

Until after World War II, professional baseball was exclusively played in the East. Ten American cities hosted major-league franchises. In contrast, minor-league teams played in towns and cities across the country; they were affiliated with major-league clubs in the East. The Minneapolis Millers were home owned during most of the team's history. They were not only a farm team for a major-league team's player development but also provided paid entertainment and were a source of taxes for municipalities.

By 1950s, Major League Baseball (MLB) teams began relocating and expanding to the West. To lure a prospective team, the Minneapolis Millers moved to suburban Bloomington. Minneapolis boosters constructed the Metropolitan Stadium. Across the Mississippi River, St. Paul business interests countered by constructing Midway Stadium for the St. Paul Saints.

The Minnesota Twins was the first professional sports team in the Twin Cities. After the Lakers left for Los Angeles, the city lacked a team. The Twins brought the national pastime, and the American League charter members Washington Senators (1901). The Griffith family determined the Twin Cities were the place to relocate from Washington, D.C. However, the American League disagreed, and compromised, since an expansion team was awarded to D.C.—and, later, departed for Texas.

But Minneapolis and the Twin Cities receiving a professional baseball team was a lengthy and hard-fought process. As early as 1952, efforts were made to attract a MLB team. At a lunch at the Minneapolis Athletic Club, Charles Johnson, sports editor of the *Minneapolis Tribune*, began his eight-year effort to bring professional sports to Minnesota with Gerald Moore, a storage and moving company businessman, and Norm McGrew from the Minneapolis Chamber of Commerce. The trio spearheaded the effort to entice baseball to Minneapolis and Minnesota.

Johnson called the Metropolitan Stadium, "The Miracle of Seventy-Eighth Street." Other hyperbolic headlines included "Triple-decked Stadium Is a Construction Miracle," and "How a Bloomington Cornfield Became a 4½ Million Dollar Baseball Stadium" in the *Minneapolis Star Tribune* on April 22, 1956, two days before the opener. He said about the concerted effort of city leaders, "It has taken four long years to make this dream come true." But the stadium was not yet finished. A fire had damaged seating along third baseline, so that entrance was not open. Tickets were $1.75 for box seats and $1.10 for the grandstand.

The new stadium elated not only the *Tribune* but also the entire city of Minneapolis, despite the location outside the city limits. Downtown

Minneapolis department stores Dayton's and Power's placed full-page ads about the Millers and the new stadium.

The Met opened on April 24, 1956. The *Minneapolis Star-Tribune* was one of the largest bondholders in financing the stadium and promoting a team's relocation to Bloomington. In 1957, the oft-rumored move of the New York Giants finally happened—but, sadly for Minneapolis boosters and fans, they moved to San Francisco. Civic boosters had hoped to sell the team on a site near Theodore Wirth Park, but residents refused. Then, another site was proposed where today I-394 and Highway 100 are located.

The Twin Cities had to wait a few more years for a team—but Minneapolis won the civic battle. The city landed the Washington Senators. American League president Joe Cronin announced on October 27, 1960, that the team would move to Bloomington. An expansion team was headed back to Washington, D.C.

The Minnesota Twins quickly developed an identity as gifted power-hitting sluggers. It was the first professional sports team named after a state—Minnesota—and not a city. Early Twins stars included Earl Battey, Bob Allison, Harmon Killebrew, Jim Kaat and Camilo Pascual. Then, in 1965, the prodigious power-hitters hosted the Major League Baseball All-Star Game at Metropolitan Stadium.

But for the 1965 season, greater things were in store. The Twins played the Los Angeles Dodgers in the World Series. Before the Twins snatched the American League pennant from the New York Yankees, the latter had won five consecutive years. Don Drysdale started the opener. As an observant Jew, Sandy Koufax refused to pitch on the High Holiday of Yom Kippur, the Day of Atonement. The Twins won the opener and game two at the Met Stadium but then traveled to Los Angeles. There the Twins lost three, including a game five shutout. Returning home, the Twins won game six, tying the World Series three games apiece. The decisive game seven was pitched by Koufax. The fire-balling southpaw threw a 2–0 shutout—the Twins lost the World Series.

The Twins continued to impress, though. Especially, future Hall of Famer Rod Carew, who slugged his way to American League Rookie of the Year in 1967. Once again, the Twins continued their winning ways when the MLB split into divisions. The team won the first American League West in 1969 and again in 1970. The 1969 Twins won the American League West but lost to the Baltimore Orioles and squandered a chance at another World Series.

In 1973, the designated hitter (DH) was introduced in the American League. The position saved the career of Tony Oliva. In 1964, the Cuban left-handed hitting slugger received the American League Rookie of the Year. Once a speedster, his body was hobbled by injuries—but his bat settled into the position.

As Oliva retired in 1976, the Twins were looking for a new home—once again, in downtown Minneapolis. In 1977, a "no site stadium bill" passed the Minnesota State Legislature: a metro-wide liquor tax was collected for the new stadium. Harry Davis was instrumental in lobbying for John Cowles of the *Star Tribune* on the site near Elliot Park.

After years of legislative squabbles and maintaining a tight budget, the Hubert H. Humphrey Metrodome opened on April 3, 1982. And because it was constructed parsimoniously, air conditioning was not installed until June 28, 1983.

In 1982, the team had a losing record and the worst attendance in baseball: 921,186. But the Twins also had a team loaded with rookies and raw talent: Kent Hrbek, Gary Gaetti and Tim Laudner were the nucleus of the team. They would go on to win the 1987 World Series by defeating the St. Louis Cardinals in seven games. The Twins gradually developed players with a strong farm system, such as pitching ace Frank Viola, and acquired key players via trade such as right fielder Tom Brunansky. In 1984, Kirby Puckett debuted, and the Twins played .500 baseball and were an exciting draw with the then highest annual attendance in Twins history—1.5 million. During the season, the Griffith family sold the team on June 22, 1984, and Carl Pohlad's purchase price was $36 million. The 1985 All-Star Game was played at the Metrodome, where the first Home Run Derby was held. In 1985, Pohlad hired "boy wonder" Andy McPhail, the architect of the team's success. He also hired thirty-seven-year-old Tom Kelly as manager.

The Twins finished with an 85-77 record in 1987—good enough to win the American League West Division. First, the Twins defeated the heavily favored Detroit Tigers in seven games to win the American League Pennant, and then they beat the Cardinals in another seven games to win the World Series. Minneapolis, the Twin Cities and the state of Minnesota erupted in celebration. It was the first major league championship since the Minneapolis Lakers in 1954. The Twins set an American League attendance record in 1988.

The Twins would experience ups and downs until 1991. In 1990, the team finished last. But with ninety-five wins, the best record in the American League, the Twins won the American League West. The team beat the Toronto Blue Jays before beating the Atlanta Braves to win a second World Championship.

In July 1996, Kirby Puckett retired after glaucoma ruined the vision in his right eye. The loss of Puckett, the team's leader, was the beginning of a string of losing seasons. In 1997, Don Beaver pursued purchasing and relocating the team to North Carolina. Following the 2001 season, Major League commissioner Bud Selig and team owner Carl Pohlad sought to "contract" the Twins and Montreal Expos. However, Judge Harry Crump ruled against contraction in November 2001. However, there was good news for Twins fans: Dave Winfield and Kirby Puckett were inducted into the National Baseball Hall of Fame in Cooperstown, New York, in August 2001.

In 2007, ground was broken on eight acres of property in the Warehouse District near downtown Minneapolis. In 2010, Target Field opened. MLB rewarded the Twins with the All-Star Game at Target Field in 2014.

The Minnesota Vikings are the city and state's favorite team. For decades, the National Football League (NFL) has been the most popular in the United States and also in Minneapolis. The Vikings consistently put a winning product out on the field, and it shows in their record. However, the team has fallen short—appallingly short—in one way: not winning the Super Bowl. Moreover, the team has not returned to the Super Bowl since January 9, 1977. The Vikings lost to Oakland 32–14 for the fourth time in Super Bowl XI.

In 1956, Metropolitan Stadium opened. The stadium was built to attract professional baseball and football to Bloomington. Both the American Football League (AFL) and the NFL competed for the Minneapolis market. Minneapolis was awarded a franchise in the AFL but later received an NFL offer.

NFL expansion teams cost $600,000 plus $400,000 in startup expenses. Dallas was awarded the thirteenth team in the NFL in 1960. Minnesota received the fourteenth franchise in 1961.

In 1967, Bud Grant was hired after Norm Van Brocklin was fired. The team's fortune quickly turned with the "Purple People Eaters": Gary Larsen, Alan Page, Jim Marshall and Carl Eller. The defensive line would transform the NFL with a prolific penchant for sacks. Quarterback Joe Kapp coined the term "40 for 60"—the 40 players on the team would give 100 percent for 60 minutes. In their first Super Bowl appearance, the Vikes lost to the Chiefs in Super Bowl III on January 11, 1970. It was the last year before the AFL-NFL merger that created the AFC and NFC Conferences in the NFL.

Then there was a big trade for the Vikings—Fran Tarkenton from the New York Giants was reunited, and he led the offense in 1972. Then, the

Vikings returned to the Super Bowl repeatedly, but never with the hardware. In January 1974, the Vikings lost to Miami. And once again, in Super Bowl IX the Vikings lost to Pittsburgh on January 12, 1975. Finally, the Vikings lost to the Oakland Raiders on January 9, 1977. The team did not return to the Super Bowl but did return to the NFC championship game, at least every decade, but never won.

After two decades using the weather to their advantage, the Vikings moved into the climate-controlled Hubert H. Humphrey Metrodome in 1982. In 1983, coaching legend Bud Grant retired. In 1984, Les Steckel was hired and then fired after a terrible 3-13 record. Grant returned for one year. Then offensive coordinator Jerry Burns was elevated to head coach.

Dennis Green was hired as head coach in 1992. He had a talented staff that included Tony Dungy as defensive coordinator from 1992 to 1997. Once again, the Vikings had another shot at a Super Bowl. In 1998, Gary Anderson, the placekicker, had a perfect season: 35 of 35 field goals, 59 of 59 point after attempts (PAT). Then he missed the field goal in the NFC Championship against Atlanta.

The Vikings' post-season woes continued in 2001. The Vikings lost to Giants 41–donut in the NFC Championship Game. Dennis Green was fired.

In 2005, Zygi and Mark Wilf purchased the Vikings from Red McCombs. The New Jersey real estate developers pushed hard for a new Vikings stadium. After years of grappling with the state legislature and the governor, they had their bill passed. In 2016, the new stadium, U.S. Bank Stadium, opened. On February 4, 2018, Minneapolis hosted Super Bowl LII.

College football as spectator sport predates professional football and the NFL. For years, college football was more popular than the professional sport. Sports were played on the day of the week available to them: Friday was reserved for high school, Saturday for college. Sunday, during the days of blue laws, the Sabbath, was all that remained for the nascent NFL and AFL.

Before the advent of professional sports, Minnesota Golden Gophers football was the most popular sport in Minneapolis. The Gophers played their first exhibition game on October 12, 1879. The intramural freshman team upset the sophomores. The game was played at the corner of University and Pleasant Avenues in the wooded area.

In 1882, the Gophers played Hamline University at the state fairgrounds in South Minneapolis. (This was when there were two competing fairs.) The game was played at Colonel William S. King's Fair Grounds located south of Franklin Avenue to the Mississippi River and south to 24th Street.

University of Minnesota Bierman Field.

Alf Pillsbury played eight seasons as a "two-way" player, both offense and defense, for the Gophers at the positions of the day: "quarter" (quarterback) and "rush line." In those years, college eligibility was not restricted by graduate school. The son of John S. Pillsbury, "the father of the University," was the captain for the 1887 and 1889 seasons.

During this time, rugby-style football supplanted soccer style as the popular version of the game. In the early decades, the rules of the game changed often, as did the shape of the field. For example, a touchdown was five points before the modern era of the game. But a few traditions were born, such as "the Little Brown Jug," which traveled with the winner of the Gophers and Michigan Wolverines game.

Around 1900, Golden Gophers football was the favorite sport in the city and state. Baseball was the "national pastime," but the Minneapolis Millers were not a major-league team. High school sports were beginning and would become popular. In 1909, one great athlete, Bobby Marshall, who excelled in baseball, football, hockey and bike racing, could participate in sports, despite his race, African American.

Bronko Nagurski was a charter member of both College Football and the Pro Football Halls of Fame. Born in Canada, the two-way player was tackle on defense and fullback on offense from 1927 to 1929. In the 1929 season,

John S. Pillsbury, the father of the University of Minnesota.

he was All-American at both positions. He played for the Chicago Bears in the NFL and also had a career as a professional wrestler.

Bernie Bierman won National Championships in 1934, 1935, 1936, 1940 and 1941. He also won six Big Ten titles. The Gophers would win only one more national title in 1960—just before the arrival of professional sports. In 1941, one of his stars, halfback Bruce Smith, won the Heisman Trophy. He went on to a pro football career with Green Bay Packers and Los Angeles Rams.

University of Minnesota Golden Gophers Basketball has had a strong local following. The Big Ten conference provides competitive games for the fanbase. The Gophers also play in the lovely and historic Williams Arena, named in honor of Gophers football coach (1900–21) Dr. Henry Williams.

Basketball arrived in Minneapolis as form of winter indoor exercise before the popularization of Minnesota as "the state of hockey." Canadian Dr. James Naismith, a physician and minister, invented "basket ball" in Springfield, Illinois. The game shared similarities with a ball game played by Mayans in the Yucatan Peninsula of Mexico but with twelve-foot-high rings for scoring and seven-man teams. The game's rules were promulgated by Naismith, with peach baskets as goals, but share few small similarities with the modern game of basketball.

The YMCA International Training School taught the new game across the nation. In Minnesota, Max J. Exner brought Naismith's basketball to Minnesota, first at Carleton College in Northfield, Minnesota, but from there it spread throughout the state.

During the early years of the program, the Gophers played at various sites. The University Armory was a 2,000-seat facility first used in the 1896 season. In 1925, the team played at the Kenwood Armory, a larger facility that seated 6,500.

Then, the Gophers moved into Williams Arena, "the Barn," at University Avenue and Oak Street. In 1927, the university paid the incredibly expensive sum of $650,000 for the facility called the "Field House." Then, the largest arena in the country, it was later officially named Williams Arena. The facility now has a capacity of almost 15,000, after renovations, but sat only 9,500 when it was constructed. In 1949, it was remodeled—the east end of the arena was for basketball and the west end for hockey.

Under the leadership of Coach Dr. Louis J. Cooke, the Gophers won four Big Ten and three national championships in the early years of the program. As one of the game's first full-time paid college coaches, his career on the bench stretched from 1895 to 1924.

U.S. Bank Stadium, home of the Minnesota Vikings.

In 1959, the University of Minnesota hired John Kundla to coach at his alma mater. He had guided the Lakers to four championships in the NBA and one in the BAA (Basketball Association of America, before the merger with the NBA). Kundla wanted to return the university to glory. As Marc Huginin and Stew Thornley said in *Minnesota Hoops*, "A new era was launched in Golden Gopher basketball in 1962 when Coach John Kundla recruited Lou Hudson." The U of M integrated, for the first time offering African American student-athletes athletic scholarships, and began recruiting nationally. During the 1963–64 season, the team added Archie Clark and Don Yates.

Since then, the Gophers team has consistently been competitive in the Big Ten, with championships in 1972, 1982 and another in 1997. The basketball squad's '97 season was vacated because of academic cheating violations sanctioned by the NCAA. Despite, the massive setback, the Gophers have appeared in the NCAA Tournament thirteen times and once, in the aforementioned erased season, in '97, in the Final Four.

Minnesota Golden Gophers women's basketball was first known as the "Lady Gophers." For the 1900–1909 seasons, the team's record was "estimated" at forty-five wins and only six losses. The lack of certainty is insightful. Recordkeeping, then, was abysmally poor, and games were not taken as seriously as sports are in the modern era. Additionally, sports—especially women's athletics—received little news coverage.

Before Title IX, the women's team was called "Lady Gophers." In 1900, they played their first game against an outside opponent, Stanley Hall Minnesota Prep School, and won. But due to discrimination, funding for women's college sports was extremely limited.

Title IX (1972) revolutionized women's college and high school sports. Part of the Education Amendment bill, federal legislation was sponsored by Senator Birch Bayh of Indiana and trailblazer Patsy Matsu Takemoto Mink of Hawaii, the first nonwhite female U.S. representative. Mink was elected to Congress in 1964. The bill called for "equity" in athletics and was signed by President Richard M. Nixon. Women's participation was guaranteed regardless of the sport making money financially for the educational institution. Federal law promulgated parity in athletic participation in Title IX. The law's impact is manifest today at the University of Minnesota; the athletic department oversees eleven men's and twelve women's sports in 2019.

Reborn for the 1971–72 season, the Gophers women's basketball team experienced ups and downs with both scheduling and coaches. Finally, in 1982, Women's Big Ten College Basketball began. Over the years, the

Gophers' women have gone to ten NCAA tournaments. They also made one appearance in the Final Four. Led by point guard Lindsay Whalen and center Janel McCarville, the Gophers' women had their best season in 2003–4. In 2005, to honor the senior Hutchinson, Minnesota native's accomplishments, Whalen's number 13 was retired. In 2018, Whalen was hired as coach.

The Minneapolis Lakers Basketball was the most successful men's franchise in the city's history. Then, the team relocated to Los Angeles.

The Minneapolis Lakers joined the National Basketball League shortly after Ben Berger, a local restaurant and theater owner, was convinced by *Minneapolis Tribune* sportswriter Sid Hartman to host an NBL exhibition game. The Detroit Gems (NBL) was later purchased for $15,000 by Berger and Morris Chalfen, the "ice show promoter," in July 1947. For the first season, the Lakers bought the contracts of Tony Jaros and Don "Swede" Carlson. Both had played for Edison High School and the University of Minnesota.

The Lakers first season was 1947–48. In the era, NBA teams' names were riddled by sponsorship: Toledo Jim White Chevrolet, Anderson Duffy Packers and the Toledo Jeeps. Max Winter, a boxing promoter and tavern owner, became general manager of the Lakers.

But the Lakers' poor record ensured the first-round draft pick. They selected George Mikan, who revolutionized the game, and were champions for three straight years. At six feet ten inches, Mikan, was the first dominant big man and superstar. Other Lakers stars included Jim "Kangeroo Kid" Pollard, who regularly dunked in practice, and Vern Mikkelsen, the number-one pick from Hamline University who won six championships with the Lakers. Then, the team had less success on the court, so they selected Elgin Baylor as the number-one pick in 1957–58 NBA draft. By then, the Lakers were exploring moving. In 1960, the Lakers relocated to sunny Los Angeles after winning the six championships.

For almost thirty years, the NBA did not return to Minneapolis. But two short-lived franchises attempted to fill the void. The Muskies of the American Basketball Association played in 1967 and the Pipers in 1968–69 at the Metropolitan Sports Center in nearby Bloomington.

Before the NBA announced expansion plans, future owners Harvey Ratner and Marv Wolfenson made unsuccessful bids on the Milwaukee Bucks, San Antonio Spurs and Utah Jazz. Minnesota's 842 city councils voted for the new team's name. By a two to one margin, the Timberwolves won over Polars.

Light rail outside the Armory.

For the 1989–90 season, the Timberwolves were awarded an expansion team in the NBA with the Orlando Magic. The franchise expansion cost $32 million. To reestablish the NBA in Minneapolis, the T-wolves hired a familiar face as the first head coach, Bill Musselman, the former University of Minnesota coach.

The team selected UCLA guard Jerome "Pooh" Richardson with the number-one pick in the NBA draft. But the Wolves played unsuccessfully until the selection of Kevin Garnett. The number-one pick, fifth overall, was chosen straight out of high school in 1995.

Garnett developed fast as a tough defender, rebounder and scorer. With seemingly unlimited competitive drive, Garnett turned the team around. It was only a matter of finding a supporting cast of teammates on the court. In 1996, the first-round selection of guard Stephon Marbury appeared to be just the right move. But Marbury was quickly dissatisfied with his status. He wanted to be the biggest star on the Wolves and requested a trade. In 1998, Marbury was traded to the New Jersey Nets. Under Garnett's leadership, the tea went to the playoffs for seven straight years until 2004–5. Longtime coach Flip Saunders also was fired. In 2007, Garnett was traded to the Boston Celtics. The Wolves, with a few fleeting exceptions, have been in the doldrums ever since, with too many poor draft picks and bad trades.

Karl-Anthony Towns is the one exception. The athletic big man is among the league's best, but Andrew Wiggins has not lived up to the hype. Veteran star Jimmy Butler demanded and received a trade. The future could be bright for the Wolves under the leadership of head coach Ryan Saunders. However, they must also find complementary players for Towns. But that has not happened yet.

The Lynx, like the Timberwolves, shared mascots that were endangered species. The Minnesota Lynx are also owned by the Wolves; Glen Taylor. But the Lynx have followed a different path than the Wolves. In the team's short history, it has become the most successful franchise in Minnesota sports.

Women's professional basketball entered the Twin Cities market long before the arrival of the Minnesota Lynx and Women's National Basketball Association (WNBA). Women's leagues attempted to bring the pro game to Minnesota but failed because of lack of financial support. The Minnesota Fillies played in the Women's Professional Basketball League (WBL) at Met Center (1978–81).

In 1999, the Lynx received a coach and several players for the first season from the Columbus Quest of the American Basketball League (ABL). The first WNBA season was in the summer of 1997. The NBA, not surprisingly,

View of the U.S. Bank Stadium from Cedar Riverside.

backed the WNBA, the league that it invested in, owned and promoted. The Lynx, an expansion team, gradually built toward a championship.

In 2003, the Lynx had a winning record for the first time. They even made the playoffs. Again, in 2004, they returned to the playoffs but lost. The team had modest success that built the base for a perennial winner.

The Lynx, led by Coach Cheryl Reeve, guard Lindsay Whalen and Maya Moore were WNBA champions in 2011, 2013, 2015 and 2017. Whalen retired and coached the Minnesota Gophers women's team in the 2018–19 season. The Lynx future became more unclear when star Maya Moore decided to sit out the 2019 season.

YOUR GUIDE TO HISTORY

The City of Lakes Loppet
(612) 604-5330
Loppet.org

Hosted the last weekend of January, the Loppet is a cross-country skiing festival that brings enthusiasts of all levels to participate in races, nighttime torchlit runs, fat-tire bicycle races, skijoring with dogs and obstacle courses.

Medtronic Twin Cities Marathon Weekend
(651) 289-7700
www.tcmevents.org

The Twin Cities Marathon (TCM) is an annual marathon in the Minneapolis–Saint Paul area held the first weekend of October. The route takes runners around the Chain of Lakes and along Minnehaha Creek, offering participants a chance to take in the fall colors in some of the nicest parks in the city.

For more information about the following teams, see the preceding chapter.

Minnesota Gophers
gophersports.com

Minnesota Lynx
lynx.wnba.com

Minnesota Twins
www.mlb.com/twins

Minnesota Vikings
www.vikings.com

11

FROM "CLOUDSCRAPERS" TO SKYSCRAPERS

Downtown Minneapolis showcases architectural modernity from the 1880s to the present. Bridge Square and the larger Gateway District were once downtown, as St. Anthony was before. The old downtown sector was abandoned as the buildings to the west climbed higher and higher into the clouds. The Gateway was renamed the Lower Loop and fell further into derelict despair, which led to a justification for clear cutting the historic downtown area, despite the presence significant buildings, for urban redevelopment.

Minneapolis's architectural modernity was defined by Le Roy S. Buffington (1847–1931). The inventor of the "Cloudscraper," the predecessor to the modern skyscraper, he is known as the "Father of the Skyscraper." Buffington presented a plan with the necessary materials in architectural journals. Skyscrapers were possible only with revolutionary modern materials. A veneer of masonry walls was attached to a steel or iron skeleton for constructing taller and taller buildings.

In 1888, Buffington patented his design. In the United States and around the world, architects mocked him, but soon they mimicked his design. Buffington also started the Buffington Iron Building Company. He sued builders for violating his patent. However, his suits languished in the courts for so long that his patent expired, while in Chicago, William Le Baron Jenney's ten-story steel-frame Home Insurance Company (1885) was recognized as the first skyscraper.

A Minneapolis skyway.

Buffington was born and educated in Cincinnati, Ohio. In 1869, he was married in St. Anthony. In 1871, he joined the A.M. Radcliffe architectural firm in St. Paul. His offices remained in St. Paul and Minneapolis until 1874.

In the 1880s, Buffington was a nationally recognized architect. He had the largest regional firm of its kind. As Murial B. Christison described in the Minnesota Historical Society magazine article "Buffington and Minneapolis" (1942), "Buffington's office in the 1880's was one of the busiest spots in town. His firm occupied a suite of rooms and employed some thirty draftsmen. So unusual was the size of the firm, and so impressive the decoration and furnishings of its offices, that they were regarded as show places and were frequently mentioned with wonderment and amazement by the press." He designed everything from mansions for Clinton Morrison (1877) and George Christian (1879) to the first mill designed by an architect, the colossal Pillsbury A Mill (1883), which cost more than $1 million to construct.

Minneapolis developed around city hall, then on the outskirts of the city in a residential neighborhood. Until the early 1980s, city hall was referred to as the "municipal building," with joint city hall and courthouse facilities. The site of city hall replaced the first city schools. In 1856, the Union School, the first educational institution west of the Mississippi River in Minnesota Territory, was designed by Robert E. Grimshaw in the Greek Revival Italianate style. In 1865, the school burned, and the Washington School, a limestone structure with a mansard roof, was built on the lot.

City hall was constructed at 3rd Avenue and 5th Street between March 2, 1887, and June 16, 1900. This time marked the passage of the bill by the legislature and the building's entire completion. As George A. Brackett said during construction, it was designed to serve a population of 300,000 to 500,000. On November 11, 1895, the county moved in. But the city was not settled in until December 15, 1902. With additional business space, the building opened with a blacksmith shop, a horse stable and "a wool brokerage."

Franklin Long and Frederick Kees were the architects of city hall and partnered together from 1884 to 1897. Long, a native New Yorker, began as a carpenter in Chicago before apprenticing as an architect. The design of city hall borrowed heavily from H.H. Richardson of Boston's Romanesque-style Alleghany County Courthouse (1884–88). The granite exterior was quarried in Ortonville, Minnesota. Two towers measured 345 feet high; the main tower stood at the center of the clock dial 231 feet above the sidewalk. City hall remained the tallest structure in Minneapolis until the Foshay Tower in 1929.

In 1974, Hennepin County relocated most operations to the Hennepin Government Center across the street. The Hennepin Government Center was constructed with Carnelian granite and cost $53.5 million in 1972. City hall's clock tower is no longer visible because of the city's vertical development.

The Foshay Tower (1929), the tallest building east of Chicago, became a symbol of Minneapolis's mercurial rise. The Foshay measures 447 feet in height. It was modeled after the Washington Monument. For over forty years, the thirty-two-story obelisk stood as the tallest building in Minneapolis on the skyline. In 1914, Wilbur B. Foshay arrived in Minneapolis. The beautiful art deco architecture was completed prior to the crash on Black Thursday, 1929. Financial fraud landed Foshay in federal prison. But first, John Philip Sousa wrote "The Foshay Tower Washington Monument March" for the August gala grand opening; then, his $20,000 check bounced.

President Harry S. Truman pardoned Foshay. In recent years, the building was renovated and rechristened W Foshay Hotel.

The Gateway Pavilion was located on a two-block triangle between Hennepin, Nicollet and Washington Avenues. The Gateway Pavilion's green space allowed lounging, with a bathroom and employment and tourist information. The pavilion represented Minneapolis's first foray into urban renewal and the national City Beautiful movement that advocated beautifying urban centers. It was inspired by the Chicago World's Columbian Exposition (1893). Local architects Edwin H. Hewitt (1874–1939) and his son-in-law Edwin Brown (1875–1930) designed the Beaux-Arts pavilion. In 1909, the Minneapolis Parks Board with the recently hired Theodore Wirth as superintendent paid $643,000 to purchase land for the one-acre Gateway Park. There were eight to nine thousand bathroom visits per day, and the pavilion attracted the unemployed, underemployed and transients riding the rails at the two nearby train stations

Annette Atkins described the area in her article, "At Home in the Heart of the City": "By 1915 or so, the Bridge Square area was home to at least five distinct cultures: the steady urban laborers—a few married, most not—who lived near where they worked; the seasonal laborers who came and went; the people who catered to these laborers; the outsiders who dropped in for a drink or something else and then went home; and the chronic down-and-outs who had nowhere else to go."

Most city leaders, including progressives, believed all denizens of the Gateway were down-and-out. At Bridge Square, the wrecking ball of urban renewal was the imperative and resulted in the first four city blocks

Foshay Tower in Downtown Minneapolis.

removed for the Gateway Park. Minneapolis's first neighborhood became the place to ignore. As Atkins said in her article, "As the city's shadow, it housed much that Minneapolis wanted to ignore—drugs, prostitution, homosexuality, and gambling."

By 1917, the Gateway District was a skid row of sorts. The Minneapolis skid row stretched from 1st Avenue N to 5th Avenue S to 4th Street and the present-day Minneapolis downtown post office. In total, it was twenty-nine blocks and included Nicollet Island, especially after urban renewal. Still, not as large as the skid row in New Orleans, which filled forty blocks.

The Gateway was located between the two major railroad stations in Minneapolis: the Minneapolis Great Northern Depot (1913–78) or Union Depot and the Milwaukee Road. Lumber millworkers were transient in nature. By 1914, Minneapolis lumber production had declined by half. From 1919 to 1920, there was a precipitous decline in lumber production, until the last lumber mill—the Carpenter-Lamb Sawmill in Northeast Minneapolis—closed.

Missions surrounded the pavilion offering alms to the indigent and poor as the itinerant and seasonal labor force, such as lumberjacks, railroad workers and farmhands, arrived at the two nearby depots, the Union and Milwaukee Road. "Bottle gangs" met and passed a bottle of inexpensive wine or other liquors in a circle until empty. In *Metropolitan Dreams*, Millett said, "By the late 1940s, part of it had become a full-blown skid row possibly the largest in any American city with the exception of the Bowery in New York." In 1958, Minneapolis received $18 million in federal money for urban renewal.

Martin and Silberman asserted, "The Gateway's 'skid row' character was clearly evident in the area's population: nearly 3,500 mostly elderly single men, and a few women or families." As Joseph Hart said in "Down and Out: the Life and Death of Minneapolis's Skid Row," "It was a neighborhood of bars, flophouses, pawnshops, and second-hand stores; charity missions and social service agencies; small-time wholesalers and manufacturers; and office buildings that had aged past their prime."

Habitués of the Gateway had limited accommodations. As the neighborhood declined, flophouses and even "cage hotels" became the norm. In Minneapolis, cage hotels first appeared as housing for itinerant lumberjacks in 1892. A typical cage hotel room was approximately six by ten feet with plywood or tin walls and chicken wire. Bathrooms were the most lacking accommodation, with one per floor. The rooms contained a bed with a dresser and little else, perhaps detailed written material on proper behavior and violations that would lead to expulsion. In 1918, cage hotels were outlawed by the city, but they continued until after World War II. The men were known for rowdy drunkenness, but as many as 33 percent were teetotalers according to contemporary statistics.

In 1953, the Gateway Pavilion was torn down. It was widely known by the pejorative "piss house." Urban renewal swept away countless Gateway businesses, as cataloged by Martin and Silberman in "The Gateway": "36 lodging houses, 41 hotels and rooming houses; 62 bars, 3.2 joints or liquor stores; 33 cafes and restaurants, 24 loan and pawn shops, 8 second-hand stores, eight church missions."

During urban renewal, between 180 and 200 buildings in a seventeen-square-block section were torn down in downtown Minneapolis. In 1966, Morison discussed the *Tribune*'s role in Gateway redevelopment. In particular, his publisher Joyce Swan "was in the forefront of the movement to transform the city's lower loop, long a skid row area of blight and obsolescence, into the handsome Gateway Center it is today." Many blocks of buildings were demolished and remained surface parking for decades. In 1973, in "Minneapolis," Barbara Flanagan described the topography: "Lakes are Minneapolis' most noticeable landmark from the air. The other, unfortunately, is blocks of unsightly parking lots….Fortunately, city planners are aiming to someday put cars somewhere else."

The grand plans for the Gateway Center were never realized. Instead, the few replacement buildings were constructed, quickly deteriorated and rapidly disappeared to the wrecking ball—and more plans for the future.

The greatest tragedy of Minneapolis's urban renewal was the destruction of the Metropolitan Building. E. Townsend Mix designed the Northwestern Guaranty Loan Building for Louis F. Menage, his final and greatest architectural achievement. The granite and brownish-red Lake Superior Sandstone exterior was 220 feet high. The building was capped by a 48-foot tower. Martin and Silberman called the Metropolitan Building "the city's first real skyscraper" and "a nationally-appreciated architectural landmark." The robber baron Menage was a real estate developer and founder of the Northwestern Guaranty Loan Company. Over $1 million was spent on the building. The interior was described by Larry Millett in *Lost Twin Cities*: "Inside was a fantasy of light and space" that included glass floors that spread light throughout what were called "light courts." The interior design included brick, terra cotta, iron and antique oak and showcased lots of iron and glass in an open atrium.

The building formally opened on May 31, 1890: "Upon invitation, 1,000 of the foremost citizens of Minneapolis and St. Paul attended this elite reception while two orchestras played music for dancing," wrote Rosheim. The balconies centered on the lobby. There was also a roof garden on the tower atop the building. It was one of the first buildings constructed with an "interior metal frame" in Minneapolis.

After the Panic of 1893, Menage's criminal finances collapsed. Fearing court dates and prosecution because of financial malfeasance, he went on the lam. Thomas Lowry purchased the building. In 1905, it was sold to the Metropolitan Life Insurance Company. For decades, the building maintained high levels of occupancy and upkeep.

Despite the excellent condition of the building and its intrinsic opulence, urban renewal became the clarion call. The Metropolitan Building was old. Even Victorian wonders stood in the way of modernity. These buildings must be cleared. The historic Gateway District buildings were considered fire traps and eyesores in the way of parking lots, freeways and widened roads.

But there were challenges to "progress," for example, from the Hennepin County History Society and the Minnesota Historical Society. The former organization lobbied the city and state to preserve the building that was "the most expensive and prominent," said the *Hennepin County History Magazine*

Eduardo Kobra's giant mural of Bob Dylan in downtown Minneapolis.

(Summer 1959). Millett wrote in *Metropolitan Dreams* that the building "would be the first great preservation battle in state history and it would rage for nearly two years amid a welter claims and counterclaims, endorsement from some of the nation's leading architects and historians, lawsuits, and even dark allegations of conspiracy and fraud."

On December 20, 1961, the arduous tear down commenced. In "Legacy of Minneapolis," Borchert described the saddest victim of urban renewal: the Metropolitan Building "had been an architectural wonder of its day—the tallest structure west of Chicago, with ornamentation and amenities that made it the object of enormous public interest." In 1961, Art Naftalin became mayor and attempted to save the building with the Hennepin County Historical Society's support. But the effort failed. The Minnesota Supreme Court upheld the Housing and Redevelopment Authority's condemnation decision. The building was scheduled for demolition and razed in December 1961.

By the end of 1963, only the federal office building, the Minneapolis Post Office and the two railroad depots remained of the Gateway. The skid row continued, by relocated to Nicollet Island and along East Hennepin, and other areas of the city.

The island was then "light-industrial" and "low-rent housing." During that time, the Eastman Flats was carved into eighty units and condemned in 1972. John Kerwin renovated the Grove Street Flats into eighteen units.

Like Nicollet Island, there were other Victorian gems just outside of the perimeter of the Gateway redevelopment project. A few were spared. Victorian architectural history was nearly wiped away, but these prime examples remain as testimony to Minneapolis's past.

The Lumber Exchange Building (1886) represented Minneapolis as a "sawdust town." The city led the nation in lumber milling from 1848 to 1887. The building was the tallest in the city and the first with ten stories in 1886, and two stories were added in 1891. One of the great extant Victorian-era skyscrapers in the city, it is another exemplar of Victorian-era Richardsonian Romanesque style. The style was characterized by sandstone with granite walls. Beginning in 1925, the Hennepin Baths were located in the basement of the Lumber Exchange Building, as baths became standard features and an accepted part of hygiene in the decades of the '20s and '30s. The basement remained a gay hangout until the building's renovation in 1979.

The Masonic Temple was renamed the Hennepin Center for the Arts after renovation, and today, it is the Cowles Center. The architects

Hennepin County Center for the Arts, part of The Cowles Center.

Long and Kees combined Victorian Ohio sandstone with columns in an Egyptian style topped by balconies and bays. In 1979, the building was renovated into art space.

The Shubert Theatre is today the Goodale Theatre and part of the Cowles Center for Dance and Performing Arts. In 1910, when the theater opened, it was one of one of the fifty-plus venues across the United States owned by Sam S. Shubert. The theater served numerous purposes over the years, showing moving and as a burlesque and striptease club. In the 1980s, the city decided to demolish Block E, and the "save the Shubert" campaign began. Over the years, the building remained alone on the city block. It was moved in February 1999 for $4.7 million. The movie theater with the terra-cotta façade that seated 1,100 was vacant for over twenty years. It was relocated from 1st Avenue and 7th Street to a site on Hennepin Avenue. Leroy Buffington's luxurious West Hotel (1884) with its four hundred rooms and eight stories was once the finest hotel in the city and occupied the site. It was demolished in 1940. The Shubert Theatre was renamed the Goodale Theatre in 2011 in honor of the contributions of Robert and Katherine Goodale.

The Soo Line Building/First National Bank (1915) is a nineteen-story skyscraper. The Beaux-Arts building was the tallest in Minneapolis until the Foshay Tower (1929). The white terra-cotta exterior makes use of Renaissance Revival style.

The Rand Tower, at twenty-six stories, opened in 1929. The art deco design includes an ornate lobby with decorative finishes and marble walls and a terrazzo floor.

Beginning in the early '70s, iconic skyscrapers stretched across the skyline. They replaced the gutted Gateway District and older downtown buildings that defined Minneapolis's past. Corporations and bank skyscrapers dominated the local economic landscape, altering the appearance of the city.

Investors Diversified Services (IDS) Center was completed in 1973. The massive fifty-seven-story blue-green glass skyscraper transformed the appearance and scale of Nicollet Mall. Crystal Court was on the street level. The retail and office building was acquired by American Express in the mid-1980s. Millett distilled the significance of the IDS Center in *AIA Guide to the Twin Cities*: "Far taller and larger than any previous downtown building, IDS Center brought a new level of modern elegance and a new scale to the city, and it has lost none of its luster over the years." The message of modernity was conveyed by standard-bearer Philip Johnson, one of the leading exponents and "starchitects" of the era with his architectural partner John Burgee.

View of downtown Minneapolis.

Wells Fargo Center—formerly Norwest Center—was the work of Argentine architect Cesar Pelli in 1989. The buildings' design echoed and paid homage to the General Electric Building at Rockefeller Center in New York City. But the skyscraper was also rooted in a local material—with plenty of Mankato-Kasota stone and accents of white marble. It was the second fifty-plus-story building in Minneapolis.

In downtown Minneapolis, the Capella Tower (formerly U.S. Bank Place) is the most recent in the trio of fifty-plus-story buildings. At fifty-six stories, the tower is topped by an illuminated crown. Since 2015, the building has leased space to the *Minneapolis Star Tribune*.

YOUR GUIDE TO HISTORY

Hennepin Center for the Arts/The Cowles Center
528 Hennepin Avenue
Minneapolis, MN 55403
(612) 206-3600
www.thecowlescenter.org

This former Masonic Temple was built in 1888. Slated for the wrecking ball in the early 1970s, it was saved by a group of preservationists dedicated to the rescue and restoration of historic buildings in downtown Minneapolis. Since it reopened in 1979, it has been the home base for a number of theater groups, including the Illusion Theatre, as well as well as providing studio, rehearsal and performance space for a number of dance and musical troupes. Each year, thousands of children and adults visit the building to rehearse, perform and take classes. It's part of a larger complex, the Cowles Center, that includes the HCA building, the modern Cowles Center for Dance and the Performing Arts and the historic Shubert Theatre.

Holidazzle
Loring Park
1382 Willow Street
Minneapolis, MN 55403
(612) 376-SNOW
www.holidazzle.com

Every Thursday through Sunday after Thanksgiving and before Christmas, Loring Park turns into a winter wonderland with lights, free movies, ice skating and as pop-up gift shops and kiosks selling food and drinks.

Minneapolis Aquatennial
last week of July—check site for times and event locations
www.aquatennial.com

The Aquatennial is Minneapolis' biggest summer event, with most activities centered on the Chains of Lakes and the Mississippi River. Canoe rentals and instruction, torchlight parades, a milk carton boat race and other activities culminate in a huge firework show over the Mississippi River, best seen from the Old Saint Anthony riverfront, Nicollet Island or the Stone Arch Bridge.

In 1940, Rudolph Willer coined the name Aquatennial. The insurance adjuster and labor union executive received fifty dollars and paid off his dental bill. "The best days of summer" was the brainstorm of Minneapolis businessmen after attending a parade for George VI and Queen Elizabeth II in Winnipeg, Canada. Having enjoyed the parade, they wanted a similar summer event in Minneapolis. It is a nonprofit supported by donations from Minneapolis businesses. The Aquatennial Torchlight Parade occurred in the first year and became an annual tradition.

Minneapolis Post Office (Downtown)

100 South 1st Street
Minneapolis, MN 55401
usps.com

The present-day post office was completed in 1933. The art deco building was constructed near the site of the first home in Minneapolis, the John H. Stevens House. When it was completed, the post office was in the middle of an industrial district with railroad tracks along the Mississippi River that delivered many goods, including the U.S. mail. Since urban renewal, the riverfront has been transformed. City leaders question the current use of the beautiful building that obstructs three city blocks on the river.

Orpheum Theatre

910 Hennepin Avenue
Minneapolis, MN 55403
(612) 339-7007
hennepintheatretrust.org

The Orpheum Theatre, originally known as the Hennepin, opened in 1921 with the Marx Brothers. The comedians brought in more than seventy thousand guests in the first week. Billed as the largest vaudeville house in the country, it became a major outlet for such entertainers as Jack Benny, George Burns and Fanny Brice.

In 1988, the Minneapolis Community Development Agency purchased the Orpheum from singer Bob Dylan and his brother, David Zimmerman, who had owned the theater from 1979 to 1988. The Orpheum underwent similar renovations as the State and the Pantages, including extending the stage to accommodate larger performance companies. In 1993, the theater reopened to the public. Since then, the pre-Broadway world premiere of Disney's *The Lion King* and the national tour premiere of *Elton John and Tim Rice's Aida* appeared at the theater.

Pantages Theatre

710 Hennepin Ave
Minneapolis, MN 55403
(612) 339-7007
hennepintheatretrust.org

The Pantages opened in 1916 as a vaudeville house. It was part of Greek immigrant and impresario Alexander Pantages's renowned consortia of theaters. In 1922, it was remodeled by theater architect Marcus Priteca/

RKO, and a new stained-glass dome was added. It remains among the Pantages's most lovely features. In 1961, Ted Mann purchased the Pantages and operated it as the Mann Theatre until 1982.

After the Mann was shuttered in 1984, it remained closed until 1996. It was purchased by the Hennepin Theatre Trust. After a complete renovation, it opened its doors again in 2002. Once again known as the Pantages Theatre, the elegant little theater has presented music, theater and dance artists as varied as Mikhail Baryshnikov, Vince Gill and, Todd Rundgren, as well as productions by local production companies such as Jungle Theater and Chanhassen Dinner Theatres.

State Theater

805 Hennepin Avenue
Minneapolis, MN 55402
(612) 339-7007
hennepintheatretrust.org

When the State Theater opened 1921, it was considered the most technologically advanced theater in the United States. Designed by Chicago architect J.E.O. Pridmore, it was air conditioned, had the largest movie screen west of the Mississippi and had a glass stage floor that was illuminated from beneath. From 1921 to 1975, the theater was used primarily as a movie house but also hosted vaudeville acts, concerts and ballet. Now, the venue is used for live performances ranging from nationally known stand-up comic acts to musical performances from acts as varied as Mariah Carey to Disney's DCapella.

12

RENAISSANCE ON THE RIVERFRONT IN THE MILL CITY

Planning and redevelopment reshaped the once industrial nature of the Mississippi River and downtown Minneapolis. Businesses abandoned the polluted city and decaying industrial ruins, only to seem them renovated and reused decades later. The recreational riverfront was the dream of city planners and visionaries but occurred piecemeal over several decades. Anfinson posited that a "multi-use riverfront in central Minneapolis had been envisioned since at least 1917" in the *Minnesota Archeologist* 48, no.1.

The riverfront's rebirth was sparked by civic planners, political leaders and local visionaries. One such person was architect Peter Nelson Hall. He started the effort on the East Bank by renovating the Frank Pracna Saloon (1890). First, it was restored as a residence in 1969; then, in 1973, it was redeveloped as a restaurant and bar. The first rehabbed in old St. Anthony since the building's construction, it served as a saloon, warehouse and machine shop. Arvonne Fraser said in the MRROHP, "When we were first married, Main Street was known as sort of one of the most dangerous streets in the city, which is where Peter Hall then started cleaning it up." In the same oral history, Hall commented on the danger, "People were killed down there. Even after we moved in, there was a fellow called the philosopher....He looked like a philosopher, gray beard. He'd take his Social Security check and go and cash it at Surdyk's Liquor and get booze and go into the tunnel near Pracna and just sleep...live there. I think he was probably killed for money." In 1971, the eight-hundred-acre St. Anthony

View of downtown from Art Bridge.

Falls Historic District was placed on the National Register of Historic Places. The area encompasses fifteen buildings, two bridges, two natural features and one park.

De La Salle High School, the citywide Roman Catholic high school located at the center of Nicollet Island, was the epicenter for local preservation on the Mississippi River. In the 1970s, the Archdiocese of St. Paul and Minneapolis considered closing the school, while countless grads fought for the city and the river. One of the graduates—Louis De Mars, fifth ward city councilman (1971–80) and city council president from 1974 to 1980—described the impact of the academic institution in the MRROHP: "Would it be too strong a statement to say but for all these people who graduated from De La Salle or Father Moss' mafia, whatever we might call them, riverfront development might not have happened?"

Mayor Fraser took office in 1980. He said of his predecessor in the MRROHP, "I thought Al Hofstede had, while he was mayor, laid the groundwork for reemphasizing the river." Louis Zelle of Jefferson Bus Lines transformed the former Salisbury and Satterlee Mattress Firm into St. Anthony Main, then an example of the de rigueur festival marketplace style. In the 1970s, the historic preservation of such buildings occurred throughout the country, including Faneuil Hall (Boston) and Ghirardelli Square (San

Francisco). At St. Anthony Main, Zelle rehabbed in the trendy architectural style—historic properties infill buildings were combined with a rough finish. In 1985, the project expanded into the Martin and Morrison and the Upton Building (1855), the oldest commercial building in the city.

The East and West River Parkway's inception was based on ideas from a failed New Deal plan in 1938. A parkway was planned to follow two thousand miles on the Mississippi River from Lake Itasca to the Gulf of Mexico. The monumental plan, of course, never happened. But the idea was placed in Minneapolis city plans with historic precedent in Horace Cleveland's parkway system and William Folwell's Grand Rounds. In the city, gradually, slowly, the plan was completed when the Mill Ruins Park opened on the former J.L. Shiely Company site in 2001.

Meanwhile, across the river in the decaying mill district, architect Kit Richardson acquired dilapidated historic properties for Architectural Associates. In 1979, it purchased the North Star Woolen Mill and shortly thereafter the Standard Mill, or the Whitney Motel after renovation, and the Crown Roller Mill.

After the riverfront was abandoned, the MPRB recognized the historic value of a perceived dangerous wasteland. In 1988, the state legislature established the St. Anthony Falls Heritage Board stretching from Plymouth Avenue to I-35W in the south. The MPRB redeveloped the parkways, the Stone Arch Bridge, Boom Island (1987), Nicollet Island, First Bridge Park, Mill Ruins Park and the latest, owned by Xcel Energy, Water Power Park (2007).

The Stone Arch Bridge (Great Northern Stone Arch Bridge, constructed between 1881 and 1883) is an iconic symbol of Minneapolis, the Mill City. The bridge is shown nightly on the local news and repeatedly for national events like Super Bowl LII. The last train traveled across the bridge in 1981. Then city councilman John Derus saved the bridge from demolition.

A debate continued on its future use for transit and as part of a light-rail transit line or as a pedestrian and bicycle-bridge. The latter won out. It was renovated in 1994, and today, more than two million visitors cross the bridge annually. As Mayor Sharon Sayles Belton said about the bridge in the MRROHP, "You could walk. You could bike. You could Segway. You were crossing the street; it just happened to be a body of water." In the same oral history project, David Wiggins, who developed programs for the Minneapolis riverfront, said, "It became such an icon on all the news anchors' backgrounds and all the advertising....It looked like the nineteenth century again where it shows up in all the city's images. I

Boom Island Lighthouse.

think it was another case of really restoring something to its proper role in the community."

In 1963, to improve navigation, the Army Corps of Engineers replaced two spans where ships passed under the bridge. The Upper Mississippi River Harbor project began on October 5, 1948. It was located near the bridge and, eventually, extended to the terminal upriver in North Minneapolis. The path of the bridge moves diagonally and follows the western shore with twenty-three arches and is 2,100 feet long. It is the second-oldest railroad bridge on the Mississippi River and was constructed to bring the St. Paul, Minneapolis & Manitoba (later Great Northern Railroad) into downtown Minneapolis. But at the time of its construction, it was referred to as "Jim Hill's Folly."

The Upper Harbor project shut off the water power to the West Bank milling district. The remaining roots of Spirit Island were removed by the Army Corps of Engineers to build Lock No. 1 on the Mississippi River and the Stone Arch Bridge. John Anfinson wrote in "12,000 Years at St. Anthony Falls," "The Upper Harbor Project locks and dams completed the final transformation of St. Anthony Falls. An engineering marvel, the upper lock obliterated Upton Island, the site of the first hydroelectric plant and the west-side row mills. It also removed Spirit Island, where eagles had once nested. To allow modern barges and towboats to move above the falls, the Corps replaced one section of the Stone Arch Bridge with a steel truss. With the west side mills largely gone or using electricity, the Corps filled in the waterpower canal that had propelled St. Anthony to international flour-milling fame. The lock is now a dominant feature on the west bank."

In 1960, *Hennepin County History Magazine* wrote about the construction, "the most expensive phase" of the Minneapolis Upper Harbor Project. The upper lock was 400.0 feet long and 56.0 feet wide with a lift of 49.2 feet—the greatest on the Mississippi River. The lock had room for two barges and a tow boat at one trip. The three-year project cost $36.7 million. In 1960, it was 36 percent complete. The end result was the barges could travel 4.6 miles farther up the Mississippi River.

The Mill City Museum tells the city's origin story—milling. The Minnesota Historical Society explored numerous options for an interpretive center: the Pillsbury A Mill, the Crown Roller Mill, the Durkee Atwood building on Nicollet Island, the Army Corps of Engineering site and the former Fuji-Ya site, before settling on the Mill City Museum site. In 1991, the historic Washburn Crosby A Mill fire and its possible demolition were the impetus for the site's restoration and rehabilitation. General Mills

Stone Arch Bridge and former Mill District.

abandoned the A Mill complex, and the Miller Bag Company purchased the buildings for storage and eventually real estate. In 2009, in the MRROHP, Beryl Miller, the son of the owner, said, "Now, I walk around the streets, and, I'm telling you, it's a miracle. It's a miracle. If you knew this area at the time twenty-five years before this date, you'd have to say what happened here is a miracle."

Saving the mill was difficult in the age of landline telephone communications. Minnesota Historical Society director Nina Archabal, in a split second, unilaterally decided to save the mill. Archabal said, "Without having time to check with my own board or to check with anybody, I called Sharon Sayles Belton, who actually had been active on the St. Anthony Falls Heritage Board, *had* come to meetings herself, *understood* the riverfront, and *cared* about it. I got her and asked Sharon to ask the fire chief to take the hoses off the building." Archabal added, "At that point, the journey began in earnest towards the creation of Mill City Museum."

Nearby, Cedar-Riverside is a historic neighborhood with a new ethnic heritage. Once Snoose Boulevard, it has transformed into "Little Mogadishu," a Somali neighborhood. Somali culture is celebrated, such as Midnimo ("unity") at the Cedar Cultural Center and special events at the Mixed Blood Theater, Augsburg University. Between 1880 and 1910,

Cedar-Riverside contained the largest concentration of Scandinavians in Minneapolis. But, as the Scandinavian population aged or abandoned the area for the suburbs, groups of college students, folkies and, later, hippies, arrived and rented the neglected housing stock.

Before 1990, there were only twenty Somalis in Minnesota; President Said Barre abandoned Mogadishu in 1991. The United States entered Somalia when Mohamed Farrah and Ali Mahdi were in power, and the infamous "Black Hawk Down" incident resulted in the deaths of eighteen U.S. soldiers and hundreds of Somalis. On March 24, 1994, the Americans left Somalia, and clan warfare erupted in the power vacuum. One to two million Somalis escaped to find refuge in Ethiopia and Kenya.

Low levels of unemployment in the state of Minnesota made Minneapolis a destination for Somalis. The 2010 census reported thirty-six thousand Somalis in Minnesota, but community leaders believe the exact number was closer to seventy thousand.

In recent years, the Minneapolis Somali community has successfully moved into politics. Ahmed Ismail Yusuf wrote in *Somalis in Minnesota*, "A large share of credit goes to the late Senator Paul Wellstone, who in the mid-nineties first approached the Somali community asking for votes while

Cedar Riverside West.

offering his profound capacity to show care and understanding." In 2010, Hussein Samatar was elected to the Minneapolis School Board, but sadly he died of leukemia in 2013. In 2018, the Samatar Crossing pedestrian and bicycle bridge opened, linking downtown Minneapolis with Cedar-Riverside in his honor.

In 2016, Ilhan Omar was elected to the Minnesota House of Representatives District 60B as a DFL candidate and, in 2018, the Fifth Congressional District of the U.S. House of Representatives, the first Somali American in Congress. As Yusuf said, "People who survived refugee camps—now taxi drivers, hotel maids, janitors, teachers, business owners—see their children graduating from colleges, navigating the system like other Americans, and speaking English with an American accent, and they are proud of them."

Another immigrant initiated the renaissance on the Mississippi riverfront. In 1968, the Japanese restaurant Fuji-Ya was built into the boiler room at the south end of the Columbia Mill. In 1974, the restaurant was expanded into the Bassett Mill foundation. As Kimmy Tanaka and Jonathan Moore said in "Fuji-Ya, Second to None," Reiko Weston brought Japanese cuisine and reconnected "a city to its river once again." She moved to Minnesota, her husband's home state, in 1953. A Japanese immigrant born in 1935, she married a U.S. serviceman under the command of Douglas MacArthur in Tokyo. She opened the first Fuji-Ya at 9th and LaSalle Avenue. General Mills closed the Washburn-Crosby Mill and relocated to Golden Valley in 1965. But because of the liquor patrol limits (LPL), they could not sell sake—so they searched for a location near the river. Again, Tanaka and Moore said, "It was not just from the river, the waterfall, and the bridges that Weston drew inspiration, however. She saw the ruins of the 1870 Bassett Sawmill and the 1882 Columbia Flour Mill not as elements to be discarded but as artifacts to be celebrated." In 1890, it was the only remaining sawmill on the west side, and it was destroyed by fire in 1895. Weston was not bothered by structural concerns such as three-foot-thick foundation walls; instead, she incorporated them into her restaurant. The restaurant was the first sushi bar in the state in 1981.

On the former Fuji Ya site, Water Works will become the newest park in Minneapolis. The MPRB slates the opening for 2019–20. The MPRB called the Water Works the "completion of a 30-year vision" for the Mill Ruins Park. The Sioux chef Sean Sherman was selected as chef at the anchor restaurant. He and Beth Dooley authored a James Beard Award–winning cookbook in 2018, *The Sioux Chef's Indigenous Cookbook*.

Old Saint Anthony today.

Decades ago, Scott Anfinson suggested that the Falls of St. Anthony needed an interpretative center. Finally, his prediction will come true. The interpretative center and restaurant will showcase the native foraged and harvested cuisine of the region and the food of indigenous cultures throughout the United States curated by Sherman.

The transformation process along the Mississippi riverfront took decades for the MPRB, first in acquiring properties and then in the massive industrial clean-up required of the former industrial sites. Recently, invasive carp closed the upper lock, and the future of the entire Upper Harbor project and the Army Corps of Engineers role on the river are unresolved.

In 1972, Minneapolis transitioned from an industrial city on the Mississippi River to reinvent the economic and ecological goals for both. "Mississippi/Minneapolis" (1972) was one of many studies of the downtown and old St. Anthony's riverfront. The plan articulated the past, the present and the future: "The Mississippi River in Minneapolis has served many purposes. It has been a hunting ground, and a transportation artery. It has provided water and functioned as a sewer. It was the lifeblood of an age past, producing power for the mills that founded the City. It has been a barrier and yet has drawn people together."

YOUR GUIDE TO HISTORY

B.F. Nelson Park

434 Main Street NE
Minneapolis, MN 55413
(612) 230-6400
www.minneapolisparks.org

John K. Daniels's sculpture *Pioneers* was originally located in Pioneers Square across from the downtown Minneapolis Main Post Office. After sitting in a lot on Main Street NE, it was relocated to B.F. Nelson Park. The sculpture was uprooted for years but has finally found home after years of neglect. Finally, it is properly displayed after the park downtown was taken away, and it was put on a small plot across the street. Today, it is on display with the Mississippi River and downtown—an appropriate context—in the background.

Minnesota senator Amy Klobuchar, of the nearby Minneapolis Marcy-Holmes neighborhood, announced her candidacy for president of the United States at the adjoining Boom Island Park on a snowy February 10, 2019.

BIBLIOGRAPHY

Aby, Anne J., ed. *The North Star State: A Minnesota History Reader*. St. Paul: Minnesota Historical Society Press, 2002.

Albinson, Pam. *Seventy-Five Years of the Minneapolis Aquatennial*. Minneapolis, MN: Nodin Press, 2014.

Anderson, Philip J., and Dag Blanck. *Swedes in the Twin Cities: Immigrant Life and Minnesota's Urban Frontier*. St. Paul: Minnesota Historical Press, 2001.

Anfinson, Scott F. *Archaeology of the Central Minneapolis Riverfront (Part 1 & Part 2)*. St. Paul: Minnesota Archaeological Society, 1990.

Atkins, Annette. *Creating Minneapolis: A History from the Inside Out*. St. Paul: Minnesota Historical Society Press, 2007.

Atwater, Isaac, and John H. Stevens, eds. *The History of Minneapolis and Hennepin County*. New York/Chicago: Munsell Publishing, 1895.

Blegen, Theodore C. *Minnesota: A History of the State*. Minneapolis: University of Minnesota Press, 1975.

Bond, J.W. *Minnesota and Its Resources*. New York: Redfield, 1853.

Borchert, John R., David Gebhard, David Lanegran and Judith A. Martin. *Legacy of Minneapolis: Preservation Amid Change*. Bloomington, MN: Voyager Press, 1983.

Bray, Martha C., ed. *The Journal of Joseph N. Nicollet*. St. Paul: Minnesota Historical Press, 1970.

Cross, Marion, trans. *Father Louis Hennepin's Description of Louisiana*. Minneapolis: University of Minnesota Press, 1938.

Davis, W. Harry. *Overcoming: The Autobiography of Harry Davis*. Afton, MN: Afton Historical Press, 2002.

Flanagan, Barbara. *Minneapolis.* New York: St. Martin's Press, 1973.

Freshman, Phil, and Linda Mack Schloff, eds. *Northside Memories.* Minneapolis, MN: Jewish Historical Society of the Upper Midwest, 1982.

Gelb, Norm, ed. *Jonathan Carver's Travels Through America, 1766–1768.* New York: John Wiley & Sons, 1993.

Graves, Kathy Davis, and Elizabeth Ebbott. *Indians in Minnesota.* Minneapolis: University of Minnesota Press, 2006.

Green, William D. *A Peculiar Imbalance.* St. Paul: Minnesota Historical Press, 2007.

Hage, George S. *Newspapers on the Minnesota Frontier, 1849–1860.* St. Paul: Minnesota Historical Society Press, 1967.

Hart, Joseph. *Down and Out: The Life and Death of Minneapolis' Skid Row.* Minneapolis: University of Minnesota Press, 2002.

Holcombe, R.I. *Compendium of History and Biography of Minneapolis and Hennepin County.* Chicago: Henry Taylor, 1914.

Holmquist, June Drenning, ed. *They Chose Minnesota: A Survey of the State's Ethnic Groups.* St. Paul: Minnesota Historical Press, 1981.

Hudson, Horace B. *A Half Century of Minneapolis.* Minneapolis: Hudson Publishing, 1908.

Hugunin, Marc, and Stew Thornley. *Minnesota Hoops.* St. Paul: Minnesota Historical Press, 2006.

Kane, Lucile M. *The Falls of St. Anthony: The Waterfall that Built Minneapolis.* St. Paul: Minnesota Historical Press, 1987.

Karlen, Neal. *Augie's Secret: The Minneapolis Mob and the King of the Hennepin Strip.* St. Paul: Historical Society Press, 2013.

Lanegran, David A., and Ernest Sandeen. *The Lake District of Minneapolis: A History of the Calhoun Isle Community.* St. Paul, MN: Living Historical Museum, 1979.

Lass, William E. *Minnesota: A History.* New York: W.W. Norton & Company, 1998.

Lewin, Rhoda G. *Jewish Community of North Minneapolis.* Charleston, SC: Arcadia Publishing, 2001.

Mayer, George A. *The Political Career of Floyd B. Olson.* Minneapolis: University of Minnesota Press, 1951.

Morison, Bradley L. *Sunlight on Your Doorstep: The* Minneapolis Star Tribune's *First 100 Years.* Minneapolis, MN: Ross & Haines Inc., 1966.

Morris, Lucy Leavenworth Wilder. *Old Rail Fence Corners: Frontier Tales Told by Minnesota Pioneers.* St Paul: Minnesota Historical Press, 1976.

Morrison, Clinton. *The Morrisons: Minneapolis Pioneers.* Self-published, 1989.

Nathanson, Iric. *Minneapolis in the 20th Century: The Growth of an American City*. St. Paul: Minnesota Historical Press, 2010.

Rivenes, Erik. *Dirty Doc Ames and the Scandal that Shook Minneapolis*. St. Paul: Minnesota Historical Press, 2018.

Roscoe, Robert. *Milwaukee Avenue: Community Renewal in Minneapolis*. Charleston, SC: The History Press, 2014

Rosheim, David L. *The Other Minneapolis, the Rise and Fall of the Gateway, the Old Minneapolis Skid Row*. Maquoketa, IA: Andromeda Press, 1978.

Salisbury, Harrison E. *A Journey for Our Times: A Memoir*. New York: Harper & Row Publishers, 1983.

Schiffer, James Eli. *The King of Skid Row: John Bacich and the Twilight Years of Old Minneapolis*. Minneapolis: University of Minnesota Press, 2016.

Shutter, Marion D., ed. *History of Minneapolis*. Minneapolis, MN: S.J. Clarke Publishing, 1923.

Smith, David C. *City of Parks: The Story of Minneapolis*. Minneapolis, MN: Foundation for Minneapolis Parks, 2008.

Steffens, Lincoln. *The Shame of the Cities*. Mineola, NY: Dover Publications, 2004.

Stevens, John H. *Personal Recollections of Minnesota and Its People*. Minneapolis, MN: self-published, 1890.

Thornley, Stew. *Minnesota Twins Baseball: Hardball History on the Prairie*. Charleston, SC: The History Press, 2014.

———. *On to Nicollet: The Glory and Fame of the Minneapolis Millers*. Minneapolis, MN: Nodin Press, 1988.

Treuer, Anton S. *Ojibwe in Minnesota*. St. Paul: Minnesota Historical Press, 2010.

Van Cleve, Charlotte O. *Three Score Years and Ten Life-Long Memories of Fort Snelling*. Minneapolis, MN: Harrison & Smith, 1888.

Van Cleve, Stewart. *Land of Ten Thousand Loves*. Minneapolis: University of Minnesota Press, 2012.

Vang, Chia Youyee. *The Hmong in Minnesota*. St. Paul: Minnesota Historical Society Press, 2008.

Westerman, Gwen, and Bruce White. *Mni Sota Makoce: The Land of the Dakota*. St. Paul: Minnesota Historical Press, 2012.

Williams, J. F. *The Minnesota Guide*. St. Paul: E.H. Buritt & Company, 1869.

Wills, Jocelyn. *Boosters, Hustlers, and Speculators: Entrepreneurial Culture and the Rise of Minneapolis and St. Paul, 1849–1883*. St. Paul: Minnesota Historical Society Press, 2005.

Wingerd, Mary Lethert. *North Country: The Making of Minnesota*. Minneapolis: University of Minnesota Press, 2010.

Yusuf, Ahmed I. *Somalis in Minnesota*. St. Paul: Minnesota Historical Society Press, 2012.

Newspapers and Periodicals

Hennepin County History Magazine (Summer 1959)
Minneapolis Journal
Minneapolis Tribune/Minneapolis Star Tribune
Minnesota History Magazine
Minnesota Republican
Minnesota State News
St. Anthony Express
St. Anthony Falls Democrat
St. Paul Daily Globe
St. Paul Pioneer Press

Websites

Minnesota Riverfront Redevelopment Oral History Project, mnhs.org

INDEX

ABOUT THE AUTHORS

Holly Day and Sherman Wick are the authors of several books about the Twin Cities. Sherman Wick received his bachelor of arts degree in history from the University of Minnesota and has been a member of the Minnesota Historical Society for several decades. Holly Day has worked as a freelance writer for local and national publications for over twenty-five years and teaches writing classes at the Loft Literary Center.